Twelve Essential Upanishads

Volume II

Chandogya Upanishad

Teachings from the High Chant

Twelve Essential Upanishads

Three Volume Series

English translation with annotations

Shukavak N. Dasa

ISBN 978-1-889756-00-4

Volume I

Brihad Aranyaka Upanishad:

The Forest Teachings

Volume II

Chandogya Upanishad:

Teachings from the High Chant

Volume III

Taitiriya, Aitareya, Kaushitaki,

Kena, Katha, Isha, Shvetashvatara,

Mundaka, Prashna, & Mandukya

Upanishads

ISBN 978-1-889756-33-2

ISBN 978-1-889756-04-2

Twelve Essential Upanishads

Volume II

Chandogya Upanishad

Teachings from the High Chant

Translation and Annotations

Shukavak N. Dasa

श्री

SRI PUBLICATIONS

SANSKRIT RELIGIONS INSTITUTE

LOS ANGELES

SRI PUBLICATIONS
SANSKRIT RELIGIONS INSTITUTE
WWW.SANSKRIT.ORG
SAN 299-2892

LCCN 2024946386
ISBN 978-1-889756-05-9 (Hardcover)
ISBN 978-1-889756-33-2 (Paperback)
ISBN 978-1-889756-06-6 (EPUB)

Acknowledgements

I thank Dr. Vijay Arora, Ash and Nita Patel, Archana and Akhil Sheth, and Vikas Sharma and family for their generous support publishing these volumes. I also thank Robert Arconti for editing and proofreading, along with Sukulina Dasi for layout, book design, and indexing.

About the Author

Shukavak Dasa holds a Ph.D. in South Asian Studies and a Master's degree in Sanskrit grammar from the University of Toronto. He regularly lectures on Hinduism and has played a key role in the development of Hindu temples across the United States and Canada.

He has officiated thousands of Hindu weddings and performed a wide range of rituals in North America, Europe, and India. With deep knowledge of Sanskrit and the symbolic meaning behind Hindu rites, Shukavak is known for making complex traditions accessible and enlightening for diverse audiences—including both lifelong practitioners and those new to the faith.

This translation was undertaken by a Westerner who is also a dedicated practitioner of Hinduism. With a nuanced understanding of the distinction between faith and belief, and drawing from his Western education and personal spiritual practice, the author approaches these sacred texts with both reverence and a desire to find meaning relevant to a Western context. His unique perspective bridges two worlds: rooted in Western thought, yet deeply engaged with Indian spiritual traditions.

www.Shukavak.com

A Note on Transliteration and Italicization

The English alphabet has twenty-six basic written sounds. The Sanskrit alphabet has forty-six basic written sounds. That's twenty additional sounds that English does not have, which are expressed by twenty different letters. So when we try to match the sounds of one alphabet to another, if there are not enough letters to make this match, we employ a system of diacritical marks to extend the range of the smaller alphabet. For example, English has just one "a" sound. Sanskrit has three "a" sounds. So to extend the letter "a," we add two separate diacritical marks. In this way we get "a" plus two additional "a" sounds, "ā" and "ā3." Similarly, English has one sibilant, "s," whereas Sanskrit has three sibilants. In this way we get "s" plus "ṣ" and "ś". Additionally, Sanskrit has four nasal sounds while English has only one. In this way we get "n" plus "ñ," "ṅ" and "ṇ." And there are more sounds that employ diacritics, and naturally each diacritical notation has a slightly different pronunciation.

A good example of how this actually works is with the word Krishna. Properly expressed using diacritical notation, this word should be written as Kṛṣṇa. The anglicization "Krishna" is just an approximation of the sound expressed by the diacritical notation Kṛṣṇa. But who can understand the sounds created with diacritical marks without proper training? It is a difficult matter.

In this publication, in order to simplify the words for the non-technical reader, we have elected to not use diacritical notation in the case of book titles and proper names. Consequently, Ṛg Veda has become Rig Veda, the name Gārgī has become Gargi, Īśopaniṣad becomes Isha Upanishad, etc. The one notable exception is with the words *brahma* and Brahmā. When this distinction comes up, it is explained in the annotation. Following this standard we have hopefully made it easier for the non-technical reader to at least pronounce proper names and titles. Otherwise, the standard use of diacritical marks has been employed for all words that are not proper names or book titles.

As far as italicization is concerned, generally book titles are italicized. In this publication, however, in order to streamline the text, which already has so many italicized Sanskrit words, I have elected not to italicize the titles of books.

Table of Contents

Abbreviations xxii
Introduction to the Upanishads xxiii
Introduction to Chandogya Upanishad xlii

First *Adhyāya* 1

Second *Adhyāya* 25

Third *Adhyāmya* 49

Fourth *Adhyāya* 71

Fifth *Adhyāya* 93

Sixth *Adhyāya* 115

Seventh *Adhyāya* 135

Eighth *Adhyāya* 159

Sanskrit Glossary 177

Index 187

First *Adhyāya*

First Khaṇḍa 1

Om as the High Chant

Second *Khaṇḍa* 3

The Gods and Demons Quarrel
And why there is Evil

Third *Khaṇḍa* 7

The High Chant from the Perspective of the Heavens

Fourth *Khaṇḍa* 9

The Power of Om

Fifth *Khaṇḍa* **11**
Om as the Sun and Breath
Sixth *Khaṇḍa* **12**
The Union of the Rig and the Sama (1)
Seventh *Khaṇḍa* **14**
The Union of the Rig and the Sama (2)
Eighth *Khaṇḍa* **15**
The Debate on The Foundation of Sama
Ninth *Khaṇḍa* **18**
The Debate on The Foundation of Sama (2)
Space as the Source of the Sama
Tenth *Khaṇḍa* **19**
The Story of the Poor Priest
Eleventh *Khaṇḍa* **21**
The Story of the Poor Priest Continued
Twelfth *Khaṇḍa* **23**
The High Chant of Dogs
Thirteenth *Khaṇḍa* **24**
The Mystical Meaning of Certain Sounds of the Sama Chant

Second *Adhyāya*

First *Khaṇḍa* **25**
Sama as All Good
Second *Khaṇḍa* **26**
The Sama Chant in the World
Third *Khaṇḍa* **27**
The Sama Chant in Rain
Fourth *Khaṇḍa* **28**
The Sama Chant in Water

Fifth *Khaṇḍa* **28**

The Sama Chant in the Seasons

Sixth *Khaṇḍa* **29**

The Sama Chant in Animals

Seventh *Khaṇḍa* **29**

The Sama Chant in the Bodily Organs

Eighth *Khaṇḍa* **30**

Seeing the Seven parts of the Sama in Speech

Ninth *Khaṇḍa* **31**

Seeing the Seven Parts of the Sama in the Sun

Tenth *Khaṇḍa* **33**

The Syllables of the Sama Chant

Eleventh *Khaṇḍa* **35**

The Gāyatra Sama Chant

Twelfth *Khaṇḍa* **35**

The Rathantara Sama Chant

Thirteenth *Khaṇḍa* **36**

The Vāmandevya Sama Chant

Fourteenth *Khaṇḍa* **37**

The Bṛhad Sama Chant

Fifteenth *Khaṇḍa* **37**

The Vairūpa Sama Chant

Sixteenth *Khaṇḍa* **38**

The Virāja Sama Chant

Seventeenth *Khaṇḍa* **38**

The Śakvarī Sama Chant

Eighteenth *Khaṇḍa* **39**

The Revatī Sama Chant

Nineteenth *Khaṇḍa* **40**
The Yajñāyajñīya Sama Chant
Twentieth *Khaṇḍa* **40**
The Rājana Sama Chant
Twenty-first *Khaṇḍa* **41**
The Sama Chant Built on the Whole
Twenty-second *Khaṇḍa* **42**
The Ways of Chanting
Twenty-third *Khaṇḍa* **43**
The Three Pillars of Dharma
Twenty-fourth *Khaṇḍa* **45**
The Rewards of Sacrifice

Third *Adhyāya*

First *Khaṇḍa* **49**
Honey of the Rig
Second *Khaṇḍa* **49**
Honey of the Yajur
Third *Khaṇḍa* **50**
Honey of the Sama
Fourth *Khaṇḍa* **51**
Honey of the Atharva Veda
Fifth *Khaṇḍa* **51**
The Vedas as the Essence
Sixth *Khaṇḍa* **52**
The First Nectar
Seventh *Khaṇḍa* **53**
The Second Nectar

Eighth *Khaṇḍa* **53**
The Third Nectar
Ninth *Khaṇḍa* **54**
The Fourth Nectar
Tenth *Khaṇḍa* **55**
The Fifth Nectar
Eleventh *Khaṇḍa* **56**
Where the Sun Never Rises or Sets
Twelfth *Khaṇḍa* **57**
Gāyatrī
Thirteenth *Khaṇḍa* **59**
Five Pathways of the Heart
Fourteenth *Khaṇḍa* **61**
The Knowledge of Shandilya
Fifteenth *Khaṇḍa* **63**
The Treasure Chest
Sixteenth *Khaṇḍa* **64**
The Doctrine of 116
Seventeenth *Khaṇḍa* **67**
The Life of Man is a Sacrifice
Eighteenth *Khaṇḍa* **68**
Brahma in Both the Individual and the Universe
Nineteenth *Khaṇḍa* **69**
The Sun as *Brahma*

Fourth *Adhyāya*

First *Khaṇḍa* **71**
Raikva, The Man with the Cart

Second *Khaṇḍa* **73**

Janashruti Approaches Raikva

Third *Khaṇḍa* **74**

Janashruti Speaks with Raikva

Fourth *Khaṇḍa* **76**

Teachings to Satyakama Jabala

Fifth *Khaṇḍa* **78**

The Bull Teaches

Sixth *Khaṇḍa* **78**

Fire Teaches

Seventh *Khaṇḍa* **79**

The Swan Teaches

Eighth *Khaṇḍa* **80**

A Water Bird Teaches

Ninth *Khaṇḍa* **81**

The Teacher Teaches

Tenth *Khaṇḍa* **82**

The Story of Upakosala

Eleventh *Khaṇḍa* **83**

Teachings from the Householder's Fire

Twelfth *Khaṇḍa* **84**

The Southern Fire Instructs

Thirteenth *Khaṇḍa* **85**

The Eastern Fire Instructs

Fourteenth *Khaṇḍa* **85**

The Fires Conclude

Fifteenth *Khaṇḍa* **87**

The Path to Brahma

Sixteenth *Khaṇḍa* **88**

The Two Paths Created during Sacrifice

Seventeenth *Khaṇḍa* **89**
Correcting Mistakes during a Sacrifice

Fifth *Adhyāya*

First *Khaṇḍa* **93**
Breath: the Oldest and the Greatest
Second *Khaṇḍa* **95**
The Power of Breath
Third *Khaṇḍa* **98**
Instruction to Gautama Begins
Fourth *Khaṇḍa* **100**
The Heavens are Fire
Fifth *Khaṇḍa* **100**
Rain is a Fire
Sixth *Khaṇḍa* **101**
The Earth is a Fire
Seventh *Khaṇḍa* **101**
A Man is a Fire
Eighth *Khaṇḍa* **101**
A Woman is a Fire
Ninth *Khaṇḍa* **102**
The Course of Man
Tenth *Khaṇḍa* **102**
Ways of Leaving the World
Eleventh *Khaṇḍa*11 **105**
Dialogue on the Universal *Ātmā* Begins
Twelfth *Khaṇḍa* **106**
The Sky as the Universal *Ātmā*

Thirteenth *Khaṇḍa* **107**

The Sun as the Universal *Ātmā*

Fourteenth *Khaṇḍa* **107**

The Wind as the Universal *Ātmā*

Fifteenth *Khaṇḍa* **108**

Space as the Universal *Ātmā*

Sixteenth *Khaṇḍa* **109**

Water as the Universal *Ātmā*

Seventeenth *Khaṇḍa* **109**

The Earth as the Universal *Ātmā*

Eighteenth *Khaṇḍa* **110**

The *Ātmā* is beyond Measure

Nineteenth *Khaṇḍa* **111**

The First Offering

Twentieth *Khaṇḍa* **112**

The Second Offering

Twenty-first *Khaṇḍa* **112**

The Third Offering

Twenty-second *Khaṇḍa* **113**

The Fourth Offering

Twenty-third *Khaṇḍa* **113**

The Fifth Offering

Twenty-fourth *Khaṇḍa* **114**

The Importance of Knowledge

Sixth *Adhyāya*

First *Khaṇḍa* **115**

Teachings to Shvetaketu Begins

Second *Khaṇḍa* **117**
The Creation of the World
Third *Khaṇḍa* **118**
The Three Divinities and Name and Form
Fourth *Khaṇḍa* **119**
The Three Elements: Fire, Water and Earth
Fifth *Khaṇḍa* **121**
The Composition of a Body
Sixth *Khaṇḍa* **121**
The Composition of a Body Continued
Seventh *Khaṇḍa* **122**
A Person is Made of Sixteen Parts
Eighth *Khaṇḍa* **123**
The Nature of Sleep
Ninth *Khaṇḍa* **126**
Teachings to Shvetaketu Continued
Tenth *Khaṇḍa* **127**
Teachings to Shvetaketu Continued
Eleventh *Khaṇḍa* **128**
Teachings to Shvetaketu Continued
Twelfth *Khaṇḍa* **129**
Teachings to Shvetaketu Continued
Thirteenth *Khaṇḍa* **130**
Teachings to Shvetaketu Continued
Fourteenth *Khaṇḍa* **131**
Teachings to Shvetaketu Continued
Fifteenth *Khaṇḍa* **132**
Teachings to Shvetaketu Continued

Sixteenth *Khaṇḍa* **133**
Teachings to Shvetaketu Continued

Seventh *Adhyāya*

First *Khaṇḍa* **135**
Instructions to Narada
Name
Second *Khaṇḍa* **137**
Instructions to Narada Continued
Speech
Third *Khaṇḍa* **138**
Instructions to Narada Continued
Mind
Fourth *Khaṇḍa* **139**
Instructions to Narada Continued
Will
Fifth *Khaṇḍa* **140**
Instructions to Narada Continued
Thought
Sixth *Khaṇḍa* **141**
Instructions to Narada Continued
Deep Reflection
Seventh *Khaṇḍa* **142**
Instructions to Narada Continued
Discernment
Eighth *Khaṇḍa* **144**
Instructions to Narada Continued
Power

Ninth *Khaṇḍa* 145

Instructions to Narada Continued

Food

Tenth *Khaṇḍa* 146

Instructions to Narada Continued

Water

Eleventh *Khaṇḍa* 147

Instructions to Narada Continued

Heat

Twelfth *Khaṇḍa* 148

Instructions to Narada Continued

Space

Thirteenth *Khaṇḍa* 149

Instructions to Narada Continued

Memory

Fourteenth *Khaṇḍa* 149

Instructions to Narada Continued

Hope

Fifteenth *Khaṇḍa* 150

Instructions to Narada Continued

Breath

Sixteenth *Khaṇḍa* 151

Instructions to Narada Continued

Outspoken for the Truth

Seventeenth *Khaṇḍa* 152

Instructions to Narada Continued

Discernment

Eighteenth *Khaṇḍa* 152

Instructions to Narada Continued

Thinking

Nineteenth *Khaṇḍa* **153**

Instructions to Narada Continued

Faith

Twentieth *Khaṇḍa* **153**

Instructions to Narada Continued

Resolve

Twenty-first *Khaṇḍa* **154**

Instructions to Narada Continued

Action

Twenty-second *Khaṇḍa* **154**

Instructions to Narada Continued

Happiness

Twenty-third *Khaṇḍa* **155**

Instructions to Narada Continued

Abundance

Twenty-fourth *Khaṇḍa* **155**

Instructions to Narada Continued

Abundance and Scarcity

Twenty-fifth *Khaṇḍa* **156**

Instructions to Narada Continued

Abundance is all Around

Twenty-sixth *Khaṇḍa* **157**

Instructions to Narada End

Eighth *Adhyāya*

First *Khaṇḍa* **159**

The City of *Brahma*

Second *Khaṇḍa* **161**

The Object of Desire

Third *Khaṇḍa* 163
True Desires
Fourth *Khaṇḍa* 164
The *Ātmā* as a Bridge
Fifth *Khaṇḍa* 165
Brahmacarya
Sixth *Khaṇḍa* 166
The Pathways of the Heart
Seventh *Khaṇḍa* 168
The *Ātmā* Seen in the Eye
Eighth *Khaṇḍa* 169
The *Ātmā* as the Body
Ninth *Khaṇḍa* 170
The *Ātmā* as the Body (continued)
Tenth *Khaṇḍa* 171
The Dreamer as the *Ātmā*
Eleventh *Khaṇḍa* 173
The Deep Sleeper as the *Ātmā*
Twelfth *Khaṇḍa* 174
The Pleasures of the *Ātmā*
Thirteenth *Khaṇḍa* 175
A Prayer of Release from this World
Fourteenth *Khaṇḍa* 176
A Prayer to Glory
Fifteenth *Khaṇḍa* 176
The Conclusion
Sanskrit Glossary 177
Index 187

Abbreviations

AU Aitareya Upanishad
BG Bhagavad Gita
BU Brihad Aranyaka Upanishad
ChU Chandogya Upanishad
IU Isha Upaniṣad
KauU Kaushitaki Upanishad
KeU Kena Upanishad
KU Katha Upanishad
MB Mahabharata
MaiU Maitri Upanishad
ManU Mandukya Upanishad
MS Manu Samhita
MuU Mundaka Upanishad
PU Prashna Upanishad
R Ramayana
RV Rig Veda
SK Sankhya Karika
SU Shvetashvatara Upanishad
TA Taitiriya Aranyaka
TU Taitiriya Upanishad
VS Vasishtha Smriti

Introduction to the Upanishads

Reading an ancient document is like looking through the lens of a powerful telescope. The light that reaches the telescope has traveled huge distances before it finally reaches the lens of the telescope and eye of the observer. This light may be thousands of light years old, and so the observer is looking at the way things were at the time the light first began its journey. One is truly looking back in time! Similarly, the text of an ancient document is a snapshot of how things were at the time the particular document was composed. These Upanishads are ancient religious documents first composed thousands of years ago, and therefore, as we read them, we are looking back in time, seeing the state of religious thinking and practice in India at that time. The word *upaniṣad* refers to an esoteric or secret doctrine and so these Upanishads are a collection of ancient mystical teachings from a very ancient time.

The religious writings of Hinduism are collectively grouped under what is called the Vedas. The word *veda* just means "knowledge." The word is derived from the Sanskrit root *vid,* meaning "to know." So the Vedas are literally the knowing of ancient India. Today these Vedas are in two parts, the Shruti Vedas and the Smriti Vedas. We might call these two divisions the "really, really old," and the "just old." The Shruti Vedas are described as *a-pauruṣeya,* whereas the Smriti Vedas are described as *pauruṣeya*. The word *pauruṣeya* means "man-made" and *a-pauruṣeya* means "not man-made." Man-made means writings that were composed and written by a human being. These include such writings as the Mahabharata, the Ramayana, and the many Puranas. Various human writers, such as Vyasa, Valmiki and Badarayana, are the traditional authors credited with composing and recording these Smriti Vedas. The Shruti Vedas, on the other hand, have no such human authors. They are described as works that were "heard" in the hearts of semi-divine beings known as *ṛṣis*. Generally, the Shruti Vedas command higher authority than the Smriti Vedas, even though most of modern Hinduism follows the Smriti Vedas. Consequently, the stories of Rama and Sita, including the life of Hanuman, and the words of Krishna in the Bhagavad Gita are all part of the Smriti Vedas. So too are the stories of Shiva, Parvati, Ganesha and Durga.

The Upanishads fall within the purview of the Shruti Vedas and therefore hold the highest authority. The foundations of the Shruti Vedas are the four Vedas: Rig, Yajur, Sama and Atharva. Each of these four Vedas are divided into four branches called *śakhas*: the *chandas*, the *brāhmaṇas*, the *araṇyakas*, and the *upaniṣads*. Therefore, each Upanishad is connected to one of these four Vedas. Thus, some Upanishads are connected to the Rig Veda while others are connected to the Yajur Veda, the Sama Veda or the Atharva Veda.

In general, over a hundred Upanishads are known, of which just over a dozen or so are considered the oldest and most important.

These are called the principal (*mukhya*) Upanishads. Many Upanishads are later and some are even considered apocryphal. These later Upanishads, numbering about ninety-five, are often referred to as minor Upanishads and are dated from the first millennium CE right up until the fourteenth century CE. Commentators such as Shankara and Madhva have written commentaries on just ten of the principal Upanishads, but it is common to see publications of eleven, thirteen and eighteen Upanishads. The present publication presents twelve such principal Upanishads.

These principal Upanishads were traditionally memorized and passed down orally and are considered to predate the Common Era. Unfortunately, there is no scholarly consensus on their actual date or even which ones are pre- or post-Buddhist. The Brihad Aranyaka is seen as particularly ancient by current scholarship and therefore considered the oldest.

Patrick Olivelle, a Sanskrit philologist and Indologist, gives the following chronology for these principal Upanishads:

> The Brihad Aranyaka and the Chandogya are the two earliest Upanishads. They are edited texts, some of whose sources are much older than others. The two texts are pre-Buddhist; they may be placed in the seventh to sixth centuries BCE, give or take a century or so.
>
> The three other early prose Upanishads—Taittiriya, Aitareya, and Kausitaki— come next; all are probably pre-Buddhist and can be assigned

> to the sixth to fifth centuries BCE.
>
> The Kena is the oldest of the verse Upanishads, followed by the Katha, Isha, Shvetasvatara and Mundaka. All these Upanishads were composed probably in the last few centuries BCE.
>
> The two late prose Upanishads, the Prashna and the Mandukya, cannot be much older than the beginning of the common era.

These older principal Upanishads have naturally inspired a vast commentary tradition, the most important of which are the commentaries of Shankara Acharya, whose date is generally accepted around 700 CE. Shankara wrote many works during his lifetime, perhaps the most important of which are his commentaries on ten of the principal Upanishads, his Bhagavad Gita commentary and his Brahma Sutra commentary. These are the so-called *prasthāna-trayi,* or three foundational works that form the basis of *vedānta* theology.

Vedānta was an attempt to forge a synthesis and thereby find a "final conclusion" (*siddhānta*) to the Vedas, including both the Shruti Vedas and the Smriti Vedas. It was an early attempt to unify and smooth out the contradictions within the Vedas. Shankara's version of this Vedanta is known as *advaita*, but other commentators, such as Ramanuja (circa 1050 CE) and Madhva (circa 1200 CE), have their own schools of *vedānta*, also based on the *prasthāna-trayi,* known respectively as *vaśiṣṭhādvaita* and *dvaita*. Shankara's Advaita Vedanta by far holds the greatest popularity. Many followers of *vedānta* think that *vedānta* means Advaita Vedanta. They may not know there are competing forms of *vedānta*, that Madhva's Dvaita Vedanta is diametrically opposed to Shankara's Advaita Vedanta or that both synthesize a form of *vedānta* out of the very same *prasthāna-trayi* used by Shankara. They may not realize, for example, that the famous dictum *tat tvam asi* (that you are), which Shankara so commonly quotes, can also be legitimately read as *a-tat tvam asi* (that you are not), as Madhva reads this dictum.

Unfortunately, the intense impact of Shankara and the subsequent commentators following in his line of Advaita Vedanta have so dominated the tradition as to blot out these other expressions of *vedānta*. In many ways the tradition has, in effect, been frozen to the middle of the eighth century CE, yet we forget that these Upanishads belong to an age at least a thousand years before Shankara and even more prior to the times of Ramanuja and Madhva. So even Shankara Acharya comes quite late given the age of these Upanishads, yet such total dominance by Shankara and his followers has led to a stifling of newer and more modern forms of understanding and interpretation. Upanishadic scholarship tends to be stuck on the *vedānta* of eighth century India.

But from a modern perspective, we can legitimately ask why must there even be a *vedānta* in the first place? Why try to solve the inherent contradictions that exist within the Upanishads and the Bhagavad Gita or between the Shruti Vedas and the Smriti

Vedas? Why try to smooth out the tradition? The time differences between the two divisions of the Vedas alone are immense. Of course there are going to be differences and contradictions. Even the time differences between the various principal Upanishads span centuries. Of course there are going to be contradictions. Why must a religious tradition be perfectly uniform and consistent? Is it a matter of religious faith that drives this need to synthesize and smooth out a religious tradition—that if contradictions are found, they pose a challenge to religious faith and so must be resolved?

Perhaps modern comparative religion can help us resolve this problem and move on from eighth century India. One of the great accomplishments of modern comparative religion is the distinction that can be made between belief and faith. This was first brought to our attention by the theologian Wilford Cantwell Smith, who made this distinction back in the 1960s, in his book *The Meaning and End of Religion*. There he drew the distinction that within what we call religion are actually two components, an accumulated religious tradition and religious faith itself. The architecture, music, scriptures, doctrines, forms of dress, prayers, and even foods, etc., all form what he called the accumulated religious tradition. And then lying at the foundation of this accumulated tradition is the actual religious faith itself. The two interact: Faith produces the religious tradition in the first place and then in turn is nurtured and supported by that accumulated tradition.

If we accept this distinction, that belief and faith are not the same, then we realize that what one believes, the doctrines, the creeds, the theology, etc., are part of an accumulated tradition and therefore subject to change. Even the various forms of *vedānta* are part of this accumulated tradition. Of course beliefs will change over time as our understanding of the world changes. And yet a strong religious tradition is informed by its basic religious faith, which tends not to change. If we fail to see this distinction and think that religious faith and religious belief are the same, we force ourselves to become reactive and push ourselves into extreme positions of having to justify that faith when beliefs are challenged by changing circumstances. This often pushes us into anti-intellectual positions. A challenge to one's beliefs can easily create a crisis of faith; but when one understands the difference between belief and religious faith, then beliefs can change without affecting one's religious faith.

For a religious practitioner this is a liberating idea. One becomes freed from the need to rationalize or dismiss new circumstances. In the Western world probably the best example is Darwin's theory of evolution and how that was attacked when *Origin of Species* first appeared in 1859. Darwin was a direct challenge to the Christian beliefs of the day and therefore a challenge to Christian faith. Even today the attacks and denials still continue, particularly from Christian fundamentalism, which generally still fails to make the distinction between faith and belief.

Returning to the matter at hand, the Upanishads fall within the realm of scripture, part of the accumulated religious tradition of ancient India and therefore subject to change. Yet, they are sacred writings that have inspired faith and guided the lives of millions of human beings for millennia. The magic of scripture is its ability to inspire faith and recreate itself age after age and so reestablish its relevance from generation to generation. In this sense scripture is timeless. Why should these Upanishads be frozen to a certain time, the eighth century CE, and then only by one line of interpretation, Advaita Vedanta? Scripture belongs to the ages. I view the Upanishads as valuable and sacred works that also speak to our time and beyond India. They are the product of human theology as well as Hindu theology. They are relevant religious works that belong to the whole world as much as they belong to ancient India and Hinduism. Therefore, the present translation and annotations of these principal Upanishads have been largely made without recourse to any forms of *vedānta*, including Shankara's Advaita Vedanta. I wanted a fresh start. As the astronomer looks through a telescope and sees the light that has traveled for thousands of light years, similarly I wanted to look at the light of these Upanishads, see what they had to say in their time and then see what illumination they can provide us today, in our time and place, thousands of years since their inception.

Naturally, choosing to translate this way, consciously avoiding recourse to Indian traditions and commentators, creates certain limitation as well as advantages, and I am sure there will be criticism, particularly from devout Hindus who want to stay true to Hindu traditions. But there are hundreds of translations and studies that do precisely that. I direct my critics to them. This translation has been made by a Westerner who is also a practitioner. Given my Western perspective and knowing the distinction between faith and belief, I have tried to work with these sacred texts to find relevant meaning for who I am as a Westerner schooled in the West, but who is deeply involved in India and Hindu traditions. Being freed from the constraints of needing a *vedānta,* whether in the tradition of Shankara, Ramanuja or Madhva, allows me to look at these Upanishads in a new way.

What makes these Upanishads most valuable is their universal nature. They are generally non-sectarian and therefore outside of any particular religious tradition, even within India. They are not Vaishnavite, Shaivate, or part of the Shakta traditions. In general, no specific deity is mentioned as supreme. God remains unnamed. Of course, many deities and semi-divine beings are mentioned throughout the Upanishads. The sun, the moon, wind, rain are mentioned as deities. Many semi-divine beings, such as Gandharvas, are also mentioned. But when it comes to naming an ultimate being, God, no specific name is mentioned. Later Hindu traditions, which are sectarian in nature, glorify Vishnu, Shiva or Durga as that supreme Deity, but these principal Upanishads do not.

The main word for that Ultimate Source is *brahma,* and it is repeated over and over, but it is not the name of any specific deity. The word is neuter and is derived from the root *bṛh,* meaning to roar and expand. *Brahma* is ultimate power and force, and it is described as the substratum that underlies all existence and from which all things come and ultimately return. We also find words like *ātmā, puruṣa* and *īśa* being used to refer to that Supreme Source, but again they are not names. They are simply descriptions of that ultimate force and they respectively mean "supreme soul," "cosmic man" or "lord." Other such descriptive terms are also used, but never the name of a specific deity. This reluctance to impose the limitation of naming a specific deity is what gives the Upanishads their universal appeal. They are human yearnings for ultimate meaning and therefore a part of human religious thinking. Yes, they are part of the oldest Hindu traditions, but on a higher level they are not bound by geography and historical time, or even Hinduism itself. They are human and universal teachings.

These twelve principles Upanishads can be divided into three groups according to theme and historical development. The Brihad Aranyaka and the Chandogya Upanishads are what I call the sacrificial Upanishads. By "sacrificial" I mean Upanishads that focus on the Vedic *yajña* or *agni-hotra* fire ritual as their main emphasis. They are the oldest Upanishads. Next to them are the analytical Upanishads. These include the Taittiriya, Aitareya, Mandukya, Prashna, Mundaka, Kena, and the Katha Upanishads. By "analytical" I mean Upanishads that no longer build on the Vedic *yajña* as their theological foundation, but instead take an analytical approach in their teachings. The Taittiriya, for example, analyses the fire *kośas* or containers that make up our existence in this physical world, our food container (*anna-maya-kośa*), our breath container (*prāṇa-maya-kośa*) etc. The Mandukya Upanishad provides an analysis of four states of awareness, dream sleep, deep sleep, etc. The Mundaka Upanishad even criticizes Vedic ritual as inferior and just a distraction to the attainment of *brahma*. These analytical Upanishads appear after the sacrificial Upanishads. Later still are the Kaushitaki, Isha and the Shvetashvatara Upanishads, which are the devotional Upanishads as they offer prayers to that ultimate power *brahma* for salvation and protection in this world. They are the precursors of devotion (*bhakti*) best found in an even later work, the Bhagavad Gita, which is highly theistic in its devotion to Krishna.

There are a number themes running throughout the Upanishads that will be helpful in understanding these ancient works. The first is correspondence, that elements correspond to other elements. For example, the eye of God corresponds to the sun, which in turn corresponds to the eye of man. The breathing of God corresponds to the wind, which in turn corresponds to the breath within man. The mind of God corresponds to the moon, which in turn corresponds to the mind of man. The hairs on the body of God correspond to trees and vegetation, which in turn correspond to the hair on the body of man. Similar to this is the relationship between the macrocosm and the microcosm. The sun "up there" corresponds to a sun within man. The mars "up there" corresponds to a mars within man. In fact, this is the basis of Vedic astrology: Read the heavens "up there" and you can read the corresponding celestial bodies within man. The *ātmā* or soul of the cosmos corresponds to the soul within man. The *prāṇa* or life force of the cosmos is the life force within man. This theme of correspondence pervades the Shruti Vedas, and the Upanishads in particular.

Another related theme is the relationship between the whole and its parts. This famous verse from the Brihad Aranyaka (5.1.1) best captures this relationship:

pūrṇam ***adaḥ*** *pūrṇam* ***idam*** *pūrṇāt pūrṇam udacyate*
pūrṇasya pūrṇam ādāya pūrṇam evāvaśiṣyate

That is whole. **This** is whole. From wholeness, wholeness unfolds. Taking wholeness from wholeness, wholeness remains.

Here we see the use of two pronouns, *adas* and *idam*, "that" and "this." Looking out into the universe, the Upanishad says, "**That** is whole," the universe is whole. Then looking across this world, it says, "**This** is whole," this world is whole. Yet, in ordinary thinking we might say, yes, this universe is whole, but this world is just a part of that whole and therefore not whole. Yet here we are told that not only is the universe whole, the part is also whole! Then it goes on to say, take so many parts from this whole and still it remains whole! How can this be? If I have a whole pie and I take so many slices from that pie, the pie becomes smaller, incomplete. But here not only does the pie remain whole, the individual slices, the parts, are also whole. This implies that the whole is contained within the parts–that within every part of this world the whole is lying within. On another level the "that" refers to *brahma* (God) and the "this" refers to the individual *ātmā* or soul. Therefore, find the individual soul and you can find the universal soul. This is key to upanishadic thinking.

Another theme is *yajña*, sacrifice, particularly the fire sacrifice (*agni-hotra*). The two older Upanishads, the Brihad Aranyaka and the Chandogya, as we mentioned, especially focus on this ritual. In fact, the world is compared to an *agni-hotra*. The later primary Upanishads, the analytical upanishads move away from this theme and concentrate on less ritual matters of Hindu theology, but in this earliest period the *agni-hotra* is so important that it shapes the worldview of ancient Vedic culture. Simply put, the *agni-hotra* is about power. It was the overwhelming technology of the day. Creation took place with the help of the *agni-hotra*. This can clearly be seen in the opening chapters of both the Brihad Aranyaka and Chandogya Upanishads. The Brihad Aranyaka describes the world in terms of the horse sacrifice, the *aśva-medha-yajña*, which becomes a metaphor for the universe itself. The Chandogya Upanishad praises the power of sound and the mantras used in the *agni-hotra*. Both the gods and the demons use these rituals in the form of the High Chant, the *udgītha*, as they battle for control of the world.

The *agni-hotra* was an extremely elaborate and meticulous affair that was taken with absolute seriousness. In ancient times it was controlled by the priestly class, and it was so elaborate and costly that only the royal class and certain wealthy mercantile members had access to it. It conferred power, prestige and legitimacy on the royal order. Kings were coronated and given legitimacy by the priests using the *agni-hotra*. The fire sacrifice as we know it now is called a *havan* or *homa* depending on the region of India. It is still relevant and important in the daily lives of Hindus even as it has been democratized and made accessible to the common person. Today the *havan* or *homa* is a mere shadow of the *agni-hotra* as it was practiced in Vedic times. Hindu priests regularly perform these sacrifices in temples and the homes of Hindu families. Even though the fire sacrifice has been largely replaced by devotion it is still a significant part of Hindu religious life. In the days of the Upanishads, it was not just a part of the religious life—it **was** the religious life.

Another feature of the Upanishads is reductionism. What I mean by reductionism is the tendency to reduce life to its most basic level, the "nuts and bolts" of life, so to speak: breath, food, loneliness, power, etc. The Brihad Aranyaka and Chandogya Upanishads, for example, talks of food, breath, sex and power as the foundations of life. They even talk of loneliness as a reason for creation. God, *brahma*, felt alone and so, being alone and feeling the need for an other, creation burst forth. The very language of the Upanishads is simple and basic, yet sublime! Later Sanskrit texts like the Puranas have a much more embellished and flowery language involving complicated meters and word play, etc. The concepts and language of the Upanishads, however, are as simple and basic as language can be. And yet they are subtle and a delight to read!

There is a general understanding that the Upanishads only discuss the "high and mighty," which includes discussions of *brahma*, *ātmā* and *prāṇa,* God, the soul and life force. While this is certainly true, a lot more is discussed. A person who desires political power and progeny should perform the *agni-hotra* in a certain way. One who desires the destruction of enemies should also perform the *agni-hotra* according to certain rituals. A person who desires powerful sex should similarly perform the *agni-hotra*. One who desires the heavenly worlds wherein one can find unlimited pleasure can also follow the *agni-hotra* according to certain rituals.

The Upanishads are also full of geographic and historic references. Many times kings and priests come from various places to assemble for debate and wealth. The great King Janaka creates a contest wherein he entices the learned pundits of the day with the prize of cattle and gold. Yajnavalkya, the most learned scholar of his time, immediately comes and seizes the gold, to the horror of the other pundits. He boldly declares he is there for the gold. The Upanishads reflect human nature in all its forms, base and sublime. There are references to famine and drought and floods. There are references to social ideas involving caste, kings teaching *brāhmanas*, wealthy merchants and women receiving mystical knowledge, etc. There are references to female issues, including marriage, birth control and childbirth. There is misogyny. There is humor and satire. There is a section where priests are compared to chanting dogs barking for food and drink. And of course there is great poetry, and beautiful metaphors throughout. The honey talks from the Brihad Aranyaka Upanishad are exquisite.

These Upanishads show evidence of a religious shift. Joseph Campbell spoke of different religious types, namely religions of affirmation and religions of denial. Many early religions saw this world in positive terms. These are religions of affirmation and they tend to emphasize embracing and affirming the world as it is rather than seeking to escape it. An opposite religious mode is one of denial wherein the world is seen as blatantly evil, false and unreal. Such a religious view tends to focus on transcending or escaping the world of suffering and limitations. These religions often emphasize renunciation of worldly desires, ascetic practices, and detachment from material concerns. It is common within the same religious tradition to find these different phases of religious development at different times.

Within these principal Upanishads we can see evidence of religious affirmation in the earliest Upanishads with their emphasis on the Vedic sacrifice as a means to obtain whatever one desire in this world. Life was essentially good and the sacrifice was the means to contact the gods to obtain what was necessary to live happily. There was little concerns for salvation or release from this world. The Isha Upanishads tells us how to live a hundred years enjoying this world. It is a positive affirmation of life. But later on in the same principal Upanishads we can see a shift to a religion of denial. For example, the simple words *sat* and *asat* completely reverse their meaning from the early sacrificial Upanishads to the later devotional Upanishads thus suggesting a shift in religious type. The word *sat* literally means what is real and true. From *sat* we get the word *satya* which is generally translated as truth. *Asat* is the total opposite, what is unreal and untrue. In the later devotional Upanishads including works like the Bhagavad Gita, and throughout the *smriti* tradition, *sat* refers to God (*brahma*) and the soul (*ātmā*), whereas this physical world including the body are called *asat*, unreal and temporary. In other words, spiritual "things" are *sat* and physical "things" are *asat*. Yet in the early sacrificial Upanishads, especially the Brihad Aranyaka Upanishad *sat* is used to refer to this physical world while *asat* is used to refer to the unseen spiritual realm "up there" so to speak. And this makes good sense. This physical reality, what we see before us, **is** real. You can touch it, see it and walk on it. It is concrete and apparent, of course it is *sat*. On the other hand, the soul, God and a spiritual reality that may be "up there" or inside of us **is** unseen, intangible and elusive. It makes sense to call it *asat*. Referring to the world as *sat*, real and true, is an affirmation of the world. But the later shift to view the world as *asat*, unreal and false, is evidence of a religious shift from religious affirmation to religious denial. In its extreme form Advaita Vedanta uses the doctrine of illusion (*māyā*) to sees this world as false and something to become free from.

The Upanishads are therefore much more than simply theological documents. They are historical works, they are literature, and, most important of all, they are human documents. They arose within India and are the product of Hindu thought, yet they easily rise to the level of world theology, world literature, and world scripture.

Chandogya Upanishad

Introduction to

Chandogya Upanishad

The Chandogya Upanishad is the second of the two major Upanishads, the first and oldest being the Brihad Aranyaka, the Great Forest Upanishad. While the Brihad Aranyaka belongs to the Yajur Veda, the Chandogya belongs to the Sama Veda and can be dated somewhat later than the Brihad Aranyaka. Literally, "*chāndogya*" means the "singer of the *chandas*," *chandas* being the hymns of the Sama Veda, and *gya* means to sing (derived from *gai* to sing). This Upanishad is also part of the Chandogya Brahmana. Here the singer is the *Udgātṛ* priest. In a Vedic *yajña* there are four head priests each representing one of the Vedas. The *Udgātṛ* is the Sama Veda priest. The central theme of this Upanishad is the correspondence between the cosmos and the fire ritual as it is fashioned around the High Chant. This work therefore opens with a discussion of the High Chant, the *udgītha*, which is a central theme of the Sama Veda. That the Chandogya and the Brihad Aranyaka Upanishads include identical sections and stories suggests that both are coming from a common Upanishadic source.

First *Adhyāya*[1]

The Glorification of Sama Chanting[2]

First *Khaṇḍa*

Om as the High Chant

1. This syllable *Om* is venerated[3] as much as the High Chant[4] itself. Indeed, it is the same as the High Chant because one sings the High Chant beginning with *Om*. Here is the explanation.[5]

2-3. Earth is the very essence of all elements.[6] Water is the essence of earth. Living beings[7] are the essence of water. Man is

---

[1] As the BU was divided into Adhyāyas and Brāhmaṇas, major and minor sections, this Upanishad is divided into Adhyāyas and Khaṇḍas.

[2] The first two chapters of this Upanishad reveal a priestly worldview built around the Vedic Fire Sacrifice, particularly the *Agniṣṭoma*, which involves the Soma plant. Soma was the juice extracted from the stalk of the Soma plant that had medicinal and likely hallucinogenic properties. Agni, of course, is the fire deity, who was evoked for the fire *yagña*. This *yagña* was primarily a means of communication with the gods, the ancestors, and other elements of the universe.

[3] Literally the word is venerate or worship (*upāsīta*). One should venerate *Om* as the main chant.

[4] The High Chant is the *Udgītha*. See BU 1.3.1 fn.

[5] CU Chapters 1 through 9.

[6] The word is *bhūta,* which can mean "things" in general or the prime elements, such as earth, water, fire, etc.

[7] The word is *oṣadhayah*, which literally means "plants." Here it has been glossed as "living things."

the essence of living beings. Speech is the essence of man. The Rig is the essence of speech. The Sama is the essence of the Rig. The High Chant is the essence of the Sama. This High Chant is therefore the very essence of all things. It is the supreme and most excellent of the eight.[8]

4. What is the Rig? What is the Sama? What is the High Chant? These things have been considered in detail.

5-7. The Rig is speech, the Sama is breath, and the syllable *Om* is the High Chant. Thus speech and breath, Rig and Sama, are a couple, and in their union the syllable *Om* is produced. When this couple comes together, they mutually fulfill each other. One who knows this and understands that the High Chant and the

---

[8] "The eight" means the eighth in the succession of essences noted above.

[9] This is similar to saying "Amen."

[10] The *Adhvaryu,* the *Hotṛ,* and the *Udgātṛ* priests are the three main priests at a *yajña.* Each of these priests is, respectively, a specialist in the Yajur, Rig and Sama Vedas. In addition to this there was a fourth priest, the *Brahma*, who was the most senior of all and whose job it was to oversee and correct any errors and keep the *yajña* running smoothly. Each of the three priests had their many assistants. Thus the *Brahma* priest was like the orchestra conductor.

[11] There is another version of this story in BU 1.3. This is the perennial struggle between good and evil, *dharma* and *adharma,* raging within every man. The gods are the disciplined mind and senses, and the demons are the undisciplined mind and senses. Stories throughout the early and later Vedas describe this struggle between the gods and demons, the *devas* and the *asuras*.

syllable *Om* are the same becomes one who receives pleasure.

8. Indeed, this syllable *Om* is an affirmation.[9] One says "*Om*" when one affirms something. Indeed, affirmation is prosperity! One who knows this and understands that the High Chant and the syllable *Om* are the same becomes one who gives pleasure.

9. Through this syllable the three branches of sacrificial knowledge arise. When the *Adhvaryu* priest calls, he says "*Om*." When the *Hotṛ* priest recites, he says "*Om*." When the *Udgātṛ* priest sings, he says "*Om*." In this way they honor the greatness and essence of this syllable.[10]

10. Both those who understand and those who do not understand use the syllable *Om*. But knowledge and ignorance are different things, and something performed with knowledge, faith and understanding is most effective. Indeed, this is the explanation of this syllable.

Here ends the first *Khaṇḍa*

Second *Khaṇḍa*

The Gods and Demons Quarrel
And why there is Evil

1. Once upon a time the gods and the demons, both sons of Prajapati the Creator, quarreled amongst themselves.[11] The gods took possession of the High Chant, thinking "With this High Chant we shall overcome these demons."

2. They thought of the High Chant as the life-force within the nose.[12] Immediately the demons pierced it with evil. And because of this one smells what is both fragrant and foul, for the nose has been pierced by evil.

3. Next they thought of the High Chant as the life-force within speech. Immediately the demons pierced it with evil. And because of this one speaks what is both true and false, for speech has been pierced by evil.

---

[12] Here the word *prāṇa* has been rendered as life-force. *Prāṇa* has many meanings depending on context. Its most basic meaning is "breath," but it is also "life-force" or even the various bodily organs, such as the "eye," etc. In this part of the chapter the bodily organs are going to be referenced. Later in this chapter the meaning will shift and the "breath" will be referenced.

[13] Here the word is *saṅkalpa. Saṅkalpa* is imagination, intention, or even mental conception. This verse could just as well be translated as "one imagines," "one intends" or "one conceives."

[14] In the preceding verses the word *prāṇa* has been used to mean the various bodily organs and functions, such as the eye, speech, the mind, etc., but here the basic meaning of "breath" is indicated. The full expression is *mukhyaḥ prāṇaḥ. Mukhya* means both "main" and "in the mouth."

[15] Compare this to BU 1.3.7.

[16] The other senses and functions, the eye, ear, nose, etc., only function for themselves. The "breath within the mouth," the main *prāṇa*, functions to nourish all the senses and other bodily functions.

[17] The idea is that at the end, at death, the mouth is left open because the vital functions leave through the mouth in an attempt to recover that main breath.

4. They thought of the High Chant as the life-force within the eye. Immediately the demons pierced it with evil. And because of this one sees what is both beautiful and ugly, for the eye has been pierced by evil.

5. They thought of the High Chant as the life-force within the ear. Immediately the demons pierced it with evil. And because of this one hears what is both pleasing and unpleasing, for the ear has been pierced by evil.

6. They thought of the High Chant as the life-force within the mind. Immediately the demons pierced it with evil. And because of this one thinks[13] of what is both good and bad, for the mind has been pierced by evil.

7. And, finally, they thought of the High Chant as the main breath within the mouth.[14] Immediately the demons rushed towards it to pierce it with evil, but they were destroyed, just as a clod of earth is smashed when it is thrown against a rock.[15]

8. In this way one who wishes harm or causes injury to one who knows this will himself be destroyed as the clod of earth is smashed when it is thrown against a rock. Indeed, such a person is as solid as a rock.

9. This main breath never knows sweet or foul odors because it has never been pierced by evil. Whatever is eaten or drunk using this breath nourishes all the other bodily functions.[16] This is why, at the time of death, when that breath is no longer found, a person dies with his mouth open.[17]

10. In this way the sage Angiras understood the High Chant to be the same as this main breath within the mouth, and so people understand it as *aṅgi-rasa,* the essence of the body.[18]

11. Similarly, the sage Brihaspati understood the High Chant to be the same as this main breath within the mouth, and so people understand it as *brhas-pati,* the great lord. For indeed, speech is great and breath is the lord of speech.

12. Similarly, the sage Ayasya understood the High Chant to be the same as this main breath within the mouth, and so people

---

[18] Angiras, Brihaspati, and Ayasya are the names of famous sages. Here their names are also used for what the words actually mean. For example, *aṅga* means "the body" and *rasa* means "essence." Therefore, the word *aṅgi-rasa* can mean the "essence of the body."

[19] There is reference to Baka Dalbhya later in this Upanishad (CU 1.12). He is also mentioned in the Mahabharata, Śalya Parva 41, wherein he performs a sacrifice to punish Dhritarashtra for rude behavior.

[20] The word is *adhyātmā,* which means "with regard to the *ātmā,"* and here *ātmā* is taken as "body." This is because the context has been in reference to the various bodily organs, etc.

[21] Here the word is *adhidaiva*, relating to the devas.

[22] The sun and the main breath, *prāṇa*, are the same.

[23] That that world "out there," the external physical world, and the inner world of the individual–his body and psychology–are related is a common theme throughout the Upanishads. The previous chapter described the High Chant in terms of the body of the individual.This chapter does the same from the perspective of the external world "up there," the heavens.

understand it as *ayāsya,* what comes from the mouth.

13. Finally, when Baka Dalbhya[19] came to know of this, he became the *udgātṛ* priest for the people of Naimisha and in this way he used to sing to please them. Anyone, therefore, who knows this and understands the High Chant and the syllable *Om* to be the same will become a person who secures desires by singing.

All this is with respect to the body.[20]

Here ends the second *Khaṇḍa*

Third *Khaṇḍa*

The High Chant from the Perspective of the Heavens

Now in reference to the Heavens:[21]

1. The Sun, who shines in the heavens, is to be revered as the High Chant. Upon rising the Sun sings for all beings and dispels their darkness and fear. One who understands this dispels darkness and fear.

2. This one and that one are the same.[22] This one is hot; that one is hot. They say this one shines; they say that one shines. One is the reflection of the other.[23] Therefore, one should revere both as the High Chant.

3. One should venerate the *vyāna* as the High Chant. *Prāṇa* is

the in-breath. *Apāna* is the out-breath. The combination of the in-breath and the out-breath is *vyāna,* the held-breath. Speech is *vyāna* because one speaks without breathing in or breathing out.

4. Speech is the Rig Veda. Therefore, one recites Rig verses without breathing in or out. The Rig is the Sama; therefore, one sings the Sama without breathing in or out. And that Sama is also the High Chant. Therefore, one sings the High Chant without breathing in or out.

5. Whatever activities require strength—churning fire, running a race, or stringing a heavy bow—are done holding the breath. For this reason one should venerate *vyāna,* the held-breath, as the High Chant.

6. The three syllables of the High Chant (*udgītha), ud*, *gī* and *tha,* must now be understood. *Ud*[24] is breath, for by breath all things rise up. *Gī*[25] is voice, for by voice words are formed.

---

[24] *Ud* is a prefix to verbs and nouns that generally indicates superiority, motion upwards, and preeminence.

[25] The root *gi* means to sing.

[26] The root *tha* means to eat.

[27] Literally, one becomes a possessor and giver of food.

[28] Each Vedic hymn is associated with a meter, a *ṛṣi*, a divinity, and a direction. In order to receive the result, the chanter must keep all of these factors in mind, and so the chanter is recommended to concentrate and respect each of these factors.

[29] The High Chant is the *Udgītha*. See BU 1.3.1 fn and CU 1.1.

Tha[26] is food, for by food all beings exist.

7. The syllable *ud* is heaven. The syllable *gī* is the sky. The syllable *tha* is the earth. The syllable *ud* is the sun. The syllable *gī* is the wind. The syllable *tha* is fire. The syllable *ud* is the Sama. The syllable *gī* is the Yajur. The syllable *tha* is the Rig. For one who understands and venerates these three syllables, the High Chant yields its very essence, the milk of speech. Such a one prospers.[27]

8-12. Here is how desires can be fulfilled: As one performs this sacred ritual, the following factors should be considered.[28] One should focus on and respect the Sama hymn from which one is going to sing. Similarly, one should focus on and respect the Rig verse which supplies the lyrics, the *ṛṣi* who is the poet, the divinity whom one is going to praise, the meter that one is going to sing, the hymn-form that one is going to employ, and the direction that one is going to face. Finally, one must focus on one's self and concentrate on one's desire as he recites. In this way one can expect his wish to be fulfilled. Indeed, one's wish will be fulfilled!

Here ends the third *Khanda*

Fourth *Khaṇḍa*

The Power of *Om*

1. This syllable–*Om*–is venerated as much as the High Chant[29] itself. Indeed, it is the same as the High Chant because one sings

the High Chant beginning with *Om*. Here is the explanation.

2. The gods, fearing death, took shelter of the Vedas[30] by covering themselves with the hymns.[31] And since they covered themselves with hymns, these hymns are called *chandas,* coverings.[32]

3. But even so, death could still see the gods hidden within the Rig, Sama and Yajur Vedas just as a fish can be seen in water. When the gods realized this, they emerged from the Vedas and took shelter of sound alone.

4. Therefore, after one has finished reciting the Rig, Sama or Yajur hymns, one must vibrate the syllable *Om*, for this syllable is the sound of immortality and fearlessness. In this way, by entering this sound, the gods themselves have become immortal and fearless.

5. A person who, therefore, takes shelter of this syllable and vibrates this sound with understanding becomes immortal and

---

[30] Literally, it says they "resorted to the threefold knowledge," meaning the rituals of the three Vedas.

[31] Here the word is *chandas*, which are the Vedic hymns.

[32] The word *chandas* comes from the verbal base *chad,* which means to cover. Because the *devas* covered themselves with these metrical hymns in order to avoid death, these hymns are called the *chandas*. The name of this Upanishad, *chāndogya*, refers to the *chandas* or hymns of the Sama Veda.

[33] Here the word *praṇava* is used for *om*. In the Rig *om* is called *praṇava*. In the Sama *om* is called *udgītha*.

fearless like the gods.

Here ends the fourth *Khaṇḍa*

Fifth *Khaṇḍa*

Om as the Sun and Breath

1. Indeed! The High Chant and *Om*[33] are the same! What is *udgītha* is *Om,* and what is *Om* is *udgītha.* The sun on high is both the High Chant and *Om*, for as the sun moves in space, it resonates with the sound *Om.*

2. Here is what the sage Kaushitaki once told his son: "I sang only for the sun, and so I have only you as my son. But if you sing for all of its rays, you will have many sons!"

This is with respect to the heavens.

3. Now, with respect to the body: One should revere the High Chant as the main breath within the mouth, for, as it moves, it resonates with the sound *Om.*

4. Here is what the sage Kaushitaki once told his son: "I sang only for the main breath within the mouth and so I have only you as my son. But you must sing for breath in all of its diversity and think, 'I will have many!'"

5. Indeed! The High Chant and *Om* are the same! What is *udgītha* is *Om* and what is *Om* is *udgītha*. For this reason, a pri-

est who understands[34] this can correct a mantra that was been mispronounced during a sacrifice.

Here ends the fifth *Khaṇḍa*

Sixth *Khaṇḍa*

The Union of the Rig and the Sama (1)

1. The Rig is the earth. The Sama is fire. The Sama rests on the Rig;[35] therefore, it is sung with the support of the Rig. *Sā* is the earth. *Ama* is the fire. Together they make Sama, earth and fire.[36]

2. The Rig is the sky. The Sama is wind. The Sama rests on the Rig, therefore, it is sung with the support of the Rig. *Sā* is the sky. *Ama* is the wind. Together they make Sama, sky and wind.

[34] Here the expression *hotṛ-ṣadanāt,* "from the seat of the *hotṛ* priest," refers to the main priest associated with the Rig Veda, whose job it was to check for errors in pronunciation and to correct them. Technically, the *hotṛ* is not allowed to sing the High Chant. Only the *udgatṛ* can sing it. But if the High Chant is the same as *om,* then that gives the *hotṛ* the right to chant it and correct for errors.

[35] The hymns of the Rig form the basis for most of the Sama Veda hymns. The Rig Veda supplies the mantras while the Sama Veda supplies the music.

[36] There is obvious sexual imagery here. *Sā* is feminine and *ama* is masculine.

[37] The word is *nakṣatra*, which is a thirteen-and-one-third degree segment of the solar ecliptic. There are twenty-seven *nakṣatraṣ.*

[38] Here the particular color is said to resemble the reddish color on the buttocks of an ape (*kapyāsa*)!

3. The Rig is heaven. The Sama is the sun. The Sama rests on the Rig; therefore, it is sung with the support of the Rig. *Sā* is heaven. *Ama* is the sun. Together they make Sama, heaven and sun.

4. The Rig is the lunar mansions.[37] The Sama is the moon. The Sama rests on the Rig; therefore, it is sung with the support of the Rig. *Sā* is a lunar mansion. *Ama* is the moon. Together they make Sama, the lunar mansions and the moon.

5. The Rig is light, the brilliance of the sun. The Sama is dark, exceedingly black. The Sama rests on the Rig; therefore, it is sung with the support of the Rig.

6. *Sā* is light, the brilliance of the sun. *Ama* is dark, exceedingly black. Together they make Sama, light and dark. There is a dazzling person at the center of the sun, with golden hair and beard. He shines in all brilliance, right down to the tips of his fingers.

7. His eyes are the color of the red lotus.[38] His name is elevated, and he sits above all evil. Indeed, one who know this also rises above all evil.

8. The Rig and the Sama are his songs. He is both the High Chant and the chanter. He is the lord of the worlds beyond the sun and he rules over the desire of the gods.

This is from the perspective of the heavens.

Here ends the Sixth *Khaṇḍa*

Seventh *Khaṇḍa*

The Union of the *Rig* and the *Sama* (2)

1. Now in reference to the body.

The Rig is speech. The Sama is breath. The Sama rests on the Rig. Therefore, it is sung with the support of the Rig. *Sā* is speech. Ama is breath. Together they make Sama, speech and breath.

2. The Rig is the eye. The Sama is the body. The Sama rests on the Rig. Therefore, it is sung with the support of the Rig. *Sā* is the eye. *Ama* is the body. Together they make Sama, the eye and the body.

3. The Rig is the ear. The Sama is the mind. The Sama rests on the Rig. Therefore, it is sung with the support of the Rig. *Sā* is the ear. *Ama* is the mind. Together they make Sama, ear and mind.

4. The Rig is light, the brilliance of the eye. The Sama is dark, exceedingly black. The Sama rests on the Rig. Therefore, it is sung with the support of the Rig. *Sā* is light, the brilliance of the eye. *Ama* is dark, exceedingly black. Together they make Sama, light and dark.

5. The person, who is seen within the eye, is the hymns of the Rig; he is the chant of the Sama; he is the recitation; he is the

sacrificial formula; he is the prayer. This one who is seen in the eye is the same as that one who is seen in the sun. The songs of this one are the songs of that one. The name of this one is the name of that one.

6. He is the lord of the worlds below the sun and rules over the desire of men. Those who sing and play the *vīṇā* sing of him and gain wealth.

7-9. One who understands this and sings the Sama sings of both. Through the former he obtains the worlds above the sun and the desires of the gods, and through the latter he obtains the worlds below the sun and the desires of men. Therefore, the high priest, who knows this, can rightly ask his patron, "What is your desire?" For one who sings the Sama with this knowledge has the power to fulfill all desires.

Here ends the Seventh *Khaṇḍa*

Eighth *Khaṇḍa*

The Debate on The Foundation of Sama

1. Formally, three men had become proficient in the High Chant, Shilaka Shalavatya, Caikitayana Dalbhya and Pravahaṇa Jaivali. They spoke to each other, "Since we have all become proficient in the High Chant, let us talk about it."

2. They agreed, so they sat together. Pravahaṇa Jaivali said,

"Since the two of you are *brāhmanas,* let me just listen as you speak."[39]

3. So Shilaka Shalavatya said to Caikitayana Dalbhya, "May I question you?"

"Of course, ask!"

4. "What is the source[40] of the Sama?"

"Sound."

"What is the source of sound?"

"Breath."

"What is the source of breath?"

---

[39] It appears that Pravahana Jaivali was not a *brāhmaṇa,* so he let the two others speak first. This was the etiquette of those days.

[40] The word *gati,* which literally means "a way," has the sense of "source." However, it could also be translated as "where does the Sama lead?" etc.

[41] "*Asau lokaḥ*" has been translated as "the world up there." In Sanskrit the pronoun *asau* has the sense of "that one over there." In contrast, the pronoun *idam* has the sense of "this one here." Throughout the Upanishads there is the idea of the world down here (*idam*) and the world up there (*asau*). In this verse the question is what is the source of water, and the answer is *asau lokaḥ,* "the world up there." In other words, the clouds up in the sky. This is where the heavens begin.

"Food."

"What is the source of food?"

"Water."

5. "What is the source of water?"

"The world up there."[41]

"What is the source of the world up there?"

"One should not ask beyond the world up there because we establish the Sama in the heavens, for heaven is the place from which the Sama is sung."

6. Then Shilaka Shalavatya said to Caikitayana Dalbhya, "Dalbhya, it appears that your understanding of Sama lacks a firm foundation. If someone who knows better were to say 'Your head will burst,' surely your head would burst!"

7. "Well then, let me learn from you, good sir."

"Indeed, learn."

"What is the source of the world up there?"

"This world down here," he replied.

"What is the source of this world?"

He replied, "One should not take the Sama beyond the world which is its foundation. We only establish the Sama on a firm foundation, for the Sama is only to be sung from a foundation."

8. Then Pravahaṇa Jaivali spoke, "Shalavatya, it is clear that your Sama is limited as well. If someone who truly knows were to say 'Your head will burst,' indeed your head would burst!"

"Well then, let me learn from you, good sir."

"Indeed, learn."

Here ends the Eighth *Khaṇḍa*

Ninth *Khaṇḍa*

The Debate on The Foundation of Sama (2)
Space as the Source of the Sama

1. "So what, then, is the source of this world?"

"It is space.[42] For all things arise from space and return to space.

---

[42] The word for space is *ākāśa*. Here *ākāśa* is used as a metaphor for *brahma* because it is infinite and all-pervading.

[43] The type of food is *kulmāṣa,* which is described as a type of fermented bean or rice dish.

Indeed, space existed before them and into space they ultimately dissolve.

2. "This High Chant is the most excellent, it is without limit, and one who understands and respects this becomes most excellent himself and prospers in these worlds.

3-4. "In the past Atidhanvan Shaunaka taught this to Udarashandilya. At that time he also said, 'Your descendants who continue to keep this knowledge will prosper in this world and in the next. Indeed, one who knows this and respects this becomes the most excellent in both this world and in that yonder world.'"

Here ends the Ninth *Khaṇḍa*

Tenth *Khaṇḍa*

The Story of the Poor Priest

1. Once, when the land of Kuru had been ravaged by hail, there lived a poor priest, Ushasti Cakrayana, and his wife, Atiki. They lived in a village inhabited by a wealthy man who kept elephants.

2. One day, as the wealthy man was eating,[43] the poor priest came begging. The wealthy man said, "I have nothing more than what I am eating now."

3. The poor priest said, "Please share what you have with me." So the wealthy man gave some of what he was eating to the poor priest and said, "Here also is something to drink."

But the poor priest said, "That would be drinking your left-overs!"[44]

4. The wealthy man replied, "Yes, but what you have already eaten are leftovers."

"Yes," replied the poor priest "But if I didn't eat that, I would die. Drinking your water, however, is optional."

5. Having eaten, the poor priest took what was left to his wife, but since she had already collected a good supply of alms and eaten, she took what her husband had given her and saved it for later.

6. The next morning the poor priest got out of bed and said, "If only I had something to eat I could go out and make some money today. I know a king who is preparing to perform a sacrifice and it is possible he might choose me as his priest."

7. So his wife told him, "My lord, we have some leftovers from yesterday." He ate that and went to the sacrifice.

8-9. He then sat by the priests and, as the first priest was about to chant, he spoke to him, "Priest, if you sing the Introductory Chant without knowing the deity, your head will burst."

---

[44] According to purity laws, the eating of food or drink from another's plate was considered impure and prohibited.

10. He then called to the second priest, "Priest, if you sing the High Chant without knowing the deity, your head will burst."

11. And finally he called to the third priest and said, "Priest, if you sing the Response Chant without knowing the deity, your head will burst." All the priests immediately stopped and sat in silence.

Here ends the Tenth *Khaṇḍa*

Eleventh *Khaṇḍa*

The Story of the Poor Priest Continued

1. The patron of the sacrifice then asked the poor priest, "My good sir, I wish to know your name."

The poor priest replied, "I am Ushasti Cakrayana."

2-3. "You, my good sir, are the one for whom I had been searching to be my head priest. But not finding you, I have chosen these other priests. Now you please become my priest."

"So be it," replied the poor priest. "Just allow those who are already here to continue to sing the prayers, but give me the same fee you are giving them."

"Agreed!" replied the patron.

4. The first priest then came close to the poor priest and said, "You, sir, had said to me, 'Priest, if you sing the Introductory Chant without knowing the deity, your head will burst.' Who is that deity?"

5. "Breath!" he replied. "Indeed, all beings take in breath when they enter this world, and they give up breath when they leave this world. Breath is the divinity who is connected to the Introductory Chant. And having been warned, had you sung this chant without knowing this, your head would have burst for certain!"

6. The next priest then came close and said, "You, sir, had said

---

[45] The reference here is to birds, who sing in the morning as the sun is rising.

[46] Here the answers have been given. Breath, the sun and food are the foundation of life. They are therefore the foundation of the Sama ritual. In other words, the ritual reflects the essential elements of life: breath, the sun and food.

[47] This chapter is sometimes called the *Śauva-udgītha*, the high chant of dogs. It has been interpreted in two ways. Primarily, it has been taken as a satire on the ritualism and externalism of the day, comparing the chanting of priests to the barking of dogs and their interest in material rewards. The other view is that this is not a piece of satire, but instead is a reference to an ancient form of asceticism wherein certain groups of ascetics would adopt the "vow of the dog." The white dog is a god in disguise, who appears before the sages in order to teach a Soma sacrifice to get food. The previous chapter made reference to famine, and so a preoccupation with food is not out of the question.

to me, 'Priest, if you sing the High Chant without knowing the deity, your head will burst.' So who is that deity?"

7. "The Sun!" he replied. "Indeed, when the sun is rising, all beings sing to it.[45] This is the divinity who is connected to the High Chant. And having been warned, had you sung this chant without knowing this, your head would have burst for certain!"

8. The last priest then came close and said, "You, sir, had said to me, 'Priest, if you sing the Response Chant without knowing the deity, your head will burst.' So who is that deity?"

9. "Food!" he replied. "Indeed, only when beings eat do they live. This is the divinity who is connected to the Response Chant. And having been warned, had you sung this chant without knowing this, your head would have burst for certain!"[46]

Here ends the Eleventh *Khaṇḍa*

Twelfth *Khaṇḍa*

The High Chant of Dogs[47]

1-3. Now the High Chant of dogs! Once when Baka Dalbhya, also known as Glava Maitreya, was on his way for Vedic study, a white dog appeared before him. Other dogs soon gathered around this white dog and said to him, "Good sir, sing for us and get us food. We are hungry!" The white dog answered, "Come and gather around me at this place tomorrow morning." So Baka Dalbhya kept watch over that spot.

4-5. The next morning they returned and filed in, hand in hand like priests coming to sing the *Bahiṣpavamāna* hymn. They took seats and began to chant: "*Om*! Let us eat! *Om*! Let us drink! *Om*! Let Varuna, Prajapati and Savitri bring us food! Lord of food, bring food! Bring food! Bring food! *Om*!"

Here ends the twelfth *Khaṇḍa*

Thirteenth *Khaṇḍa*

The Mystical Meaning of Certain Sounds of the Sama Chant

The sound *hā-u* is the world. The sound *hā-i* is the wind. The word *atha* is the moon. The word *iha* is the *ātmā.* The sound *ī* is fire and *ū* is the sun. The invocation is the sound *e*. The Vishvadevas are the sounds *au, ho,* and *i*. The sound *hiṃ* is Prajapati, the Lord of Creatures. Breath is *svara.* The sound *yā* is food, and the word *virāṭ* is speech. The thirteenth syllable is the sound *huṃ*, which is left unexplained. When this hidden meaning of the Sama is understood, speech will yield the milk of speech, its very essence. Such a person prospers.[48]

Here ends the thirteenth *Khaṇḍa*
Here ends the First *Adhyāya*

---

[48] Literally, such a person becomes both the giver and eater of food.

Second *Adhyāya*

First *Khaṇḍa*

Sama as All Good

1. Reflection on the Sama in its entirety[1] is good! Something that is good is called *sāma.* Something that is not good is *a-sāma.*[2]

2. In this regard, when people say "He has come with kind words (*sāma*)," what they really mean is that he has come with good intentions. Similarly, when they say "He has come with unkind words (*a-sāma*)," what they really mean is that he has come with bad intentions.

3. And again, when people say "We have wealth (*sāma*)!" what they really mean is that they are well off. Similarly, when people say "We have no wealth (*a-sāma*)," what they really mean is that they are not well off.

4. One who knows this and venerates the Sama as good can have all expectations that good things will come his way.

---

[1] In this section all aspects of the Sama Chant will be examined, namely the meaning of the word itself, an analysis of its five parts, and even its seven parts.

[2] The word Sama is here taken in many ways: as the name of a chant, as goodness, as kindness, and as prosperity.

Here ends the First *Khaṇḍa*

Second *Khaṇḍa*

The Sama Chant in the World

1. In the world one should revere the five parts[3] of the Sama Chant:

The earth is the mystical sound *hiṅ;*
Fire is the Introductory Chant *(prastāva);*
Sky is the High Chant *(udgītha);*
The sun is the Response Chant *(pratihāra);* and
The heavens are the Concluding Chant *(nidhana).*

2. And in the reverse order:

The heavens are the mystical sound *hin*;
The sun is the Introductory Chant;
The sky is the High Chant;
Fire is the Response Chant; and

---

[3] The five parts of the Sama, when it is used at a Soma sacrifice, are the Introductory Chant *(prastāva),* the High Chant *(udgītha),* the Response Chant *(pratihāra),* the Finale (*Upadrava*), and the Concluding Chant *(nidhana).* Here the fivefold division is different. The initial *hiṅ* (pronounced *huṃ*) of the *prastāva* is regarded as the first part, and the Finale is merged into the Response Chant. Later (CU 2.8–10) the Sama is defined as being comprised of seven parts.

Second *Khaṇḍa*

The earth is the Concluding Chant.

3. When someone in these worlds knows this and reveres these five parts of the Sama Chant, these worlds become favorable to him in both their ascending and descending order.

Here ends the Second *Khaṇḍa*

Third *Khaṇḍa*

The Sama Chant in Rain

One should revere the five parts of the Sama Chant in rains.

The wind which precedes a thunderstorm is the sound *hiṅ*.
The gathering clouds are the Introductory Chant.
The falling rains are the High Chant.
The flashing lightning and the roaring thunder are the Response Chant.
The end of the storm is the Concluding Chant.

2. For one who knows this and so reveres the five parts of the Sama Chant in rain, rains will always fall for him. Indeed, he is the cause of rain.

Here ends the Third *Khaṇḍa*

Fourth *Khaṇḍa*

The Sama Chant in Water

1. One should revere the five parts of the Sama Chant in water.

The clouds which gather are the sound *hiṅ;*
The falling rain is the Introductory Chant;
The waters which flow east are the High Chant;
The waters which flow west are the Response Chant; and
The ocean is the Concluding Chant.

2. The one who knows this and so reveres the five parts of the Sama Chant in water will never die in water. Indeed, his wealth will be water.

Here ends the Fourth *Khaṇḍa*

Fifth *Khaṇḍa*

The Sama Chant in the Seasons

1. One should revere the five parts of the Sama Chant in the seasons.

Spring is the sound *hiṅ;*
The hot season is the Introductory Chant;
The rainy season is the High Chant;
Autumn is the Response Chant; and
Winter is the Concluding Chant.

2. The one who knows this and so honors the five parts of the Sama Chant in the seasons, the seasons will always be good to him. Indeed. he will have many seasons.

Here ends the Fifth *Khaṇḍa*

Sixth *Khaṇḍa*

The Sama Chant in Animals

1. One should honor the five parts of the Sama Chant in animals.

The goat is the sound *hiṅ;*
Sheep are the Introductory Chant;
The cow is the High Chant;
The horse is the Response Chant; and
Man is the Concluding Chant.

2. The one who knows this and so honors the five parts of the Sama Chant in animals will always have animals. Indeed, his wealth will be animals.

Here ends the Sixth *Khaṇḍa*

Seventh *Khaṇḍa*

The Sama Chant in the Bodily Organs

1. One should honor the five parts of the Sama Chant in the organs of the body.

Breath is the sound *hiṅ;*
Speech is the Introductory Chant;
The eye is the High Chant;
The ear is the Response Chant; and
The mind is the Concluding Chant. These bodily organs are the most excellent of all.

2. The one who knows this and so honors the five parts of the Sama Chant in the organs of the body will obtain the best of all things and will reach the highest worlds.

This has been a discussion on the five parts of the Sama chant.

Here ends the Seventh *Khaṇḍa*

Eighth *Khaṇḍa*

Seeing the Seven parts of the Sama in Speech

1-2. Now the sevenfold division.

One should revere the seven parts of the Sama Chant in speech.

Every *huṃ* sound in speech is the syllable *hiṅ;*
Every *pra* sound is the Introductory Chant (*prastāva*);

---

[4] Two words are used here, *sama* and *Sama*. In this context *sama* means "the same," or "evenness." *Sama*, the name of the Vedic hymn, is derived from the word *sama*. In these next few chapters the idea of "sameness" in the Sama Chant will be developed.

[5] *Hiṅ* is pronounced *huṃ*. See CU 2.8.1.

Eighth *Khaṇḍa*

Every *ā* sound is the Opening (*ādi*);
Every *ud* sound is the High Chant (*udgītha*);
Every *prati* sound is the Response Chant (*pratihāra*);
Every *upa* sound is the Finale (*upadrava*); and
Every *ni* sound is the Concluding Chant (*nidhana*).

3. The words of the one who knows this and so honors these seven parts of the Sama Chant will be the milk of speech and he will become the owner and eater of food.

Here ends the Eighth *Khaṇḍa*

Ninth *Khaṇḍa*

Seeing the Seven Parts of the Sama in the Sun

1. One should revere the seven parts of the Sama Chant in the distant sun. The sun is always the same (*sama*),[4] so it is called Sama. When one says, "It faces me," and then another says, "It faces me," it is *Sama* because it appears the same to everyone.

2. One should know that all beings are connected to this distant sun. Domestic animals have their connection just before sunrise, when the sun becomes the syllable *hiṅ*. Animals, therefore, make the sound *hiṅ*.[5] They share in the *hiṅ* part of the Sama Chant.

3. At the moment the sun rises it becomes the Introductory Chant, and at that time humans have their connection with the sun. Men, therefore, desire praise and legacy because they share

in the introductory portion of the Sama.

4. Just after sunrise, at the time when cows are called for milking, the sun becomes the Opening Chant and birds have their connection with the sun. Birds, therefore, fly in the sky without support because they share in the opening portion of the Sama.

5. At high noon the sun becomes the High Chant, and at that time the gods have their connection with the sun. The gods, therefore, are the best of Prajapati's offspring because they share in the High Chant portion of the Sama.

6. After midday the sun becomes the Response Chant, and at that time embryos have their connection with the sun. Embryos are, therefore, held within and do not drop down because they share in the response portion of the Sama.

7. Past mid-afternoon, but before sunset, the sun becomes the Finale, and forest animals are connected with the sun. When they see a man, therefore, forest animals run and hide in bushes and holes. They share in the Finale portion of the Sama.

8. The setting sun becomes the Concluding Chant, and at that

---

[6] The word *hiṅkāra* is three syllables: *hiṅ-kā-ra.*

[7] The word for syllable is *akṣara*. It is made of three syllables. Therefore, it can be said there are three words, each with three syllables, and so they are all the same (*sama*).

time the ancestors have their connection with the sun. People, therefore, lay their ancestors to rest because ancestors share in the concluding portion of the Sama.

In this way one should revere the seven parts of the Sama Chant in the distant sun.

Here ends the Ninth *Khaṇḍa*

Tenth *Khaṇḍa*

The Syllables of the Sama Chant

1. One should revere the seven parts of the Sama Chant in the meter of the Sama Chant itself, which leads beyond death. *Hiṅ-kāra*–the sound *hiṅ*–is three syllables in length.[6] *Prastāva*–the Introductory Chant–is three syllables. They are, therefore, the same (*sama*), three syllables each.

2. The *Ādi*–the Opening Chant–is two syllables. The *Pratihāra*–the Response Chant–is four syllables. Move one syllable from *pratihāra* to *ādi* and they are the same, three syllables in length.

3. The *Udgītha*–the High Chant–is three syllables. *Upadrava*–the Finale–is four syllables. With each having at least three syllables they are the same. But with the extra syllable (*akṣara*) left over they are still the same.[7]

4-5. The *Nidhana*–the Concluding Chant–is three syllables. So it is also the same. In total this makes twenty-two syllables. With twenty-one syllables, one reaches the sun.[8] The twenty-first syllable is the sun. With the twenty-second syllable, one reaches beyond the sun. This region beyond the sun is the vault of heaven[9] and it is a realm without sorrow.

6. One who thus understands these syllables obtains conquest over the sun. Indeed, it is a victory even more than the conquest of the sun, for one who knows these seven parts of the Sama Chant goes beyond death. Truly, one should revere these seven parts of the Sama Chant!

Here ends the Tenth *Khaṇḍa*

---

[8] Some commentators suggest that the number 21 is comprised of twelve months, five seasons, three worlds, plus the sun.

[9] The word used here is *nāka,* which can be parsed as *na+ aka*, no pain, *aka* meaning pain and suffering. Some commentators say this is a specific place in the sky located near the zenith near the North Pole, just above the Milky Way, as seen from Northern India.

[10] Chapters 11 through 20 describe the specific kinds of Samas. This Sama *Gāyatra* is not to be confused with the Rig *Gāyatrī, tat-savitur varenyam...*

[11] There is a similar weaving metaphor used in BU 3.6.

[12] Here the word is *prāṇa* and it is used in the sense of bodily organs.

[13] There is another reference to the rubbing of the fire drill in BU 1.4.6.

Eleventh *Khaṇḍa*

The *Gāyatra* Sama Chant[10]

1. The mind is the sound *hiṅ*.
Speech is the Introductory Chant.
The eye is the High Chant.
The ear is the Response Chant.
Breath is the Concluding Chant.
This is the *Gāyatra* Sama Chant, which is woven[11] on the vital functions of the body.[12]

2. One who knows this *Gāyatra* Sama Chant becomes a controller of these functions and has a complete and long life, full of offspring, livestock and fame. But he must be broad-minded. That is the rule.

Here ends the Eleventh *Khaṇḍa*

Twelfth *Khaṇḍa*

The *Rathantara* Sama Chant

1. The rubbing of the fire drill[13] is the sound *hiṅ*.
The rising smoke is the Introductory Chant.
The fire that blazes up is the High Chant
The burning coals are the Response Chant.
The settling down and final extinguishing of the fire are the Concluding Chant.
This is the *Rathantara* Sama Chant, which is woven on fire.

2. One who knows this *Rathantara* Sama Chant becomes an eater of food and radiant in sacred knowledge and has a complete and long life, full of offspring, livestock and fame. But he must never sip water and spit before the fire. That is the rule.

Here ends the Twelfth *Khaṇḍa*

Thirteenth *Khaṇḍa*

The *Vāmandevya* Sama Chant

1. When a man first calls a woman, this is the sound *hiṅ*.
When he invites her for sex, this is the Introductory Chant.
When he lays down with her, this is the High Chant.
When he lays on top of her, this is the Response Chant.
When he reaches his climax and withdraws, this is the Concluding Chant.
This is the *Vāmandevya* Sama Chant, which is woven on sexual intercourse.

2. One who knows this *Vāmandevya* Sama Chant becomes proficient in sexual intercourse and has a complete and long life, full of offspring, livestock and fame. But he must never refuse any woman. That is the rule.

Here ends the Thirteenth *Khaṇḍa*

Fourteenth *Khaṇḍa*

The *Bṛhad Sama* Chant

1. The rising sun is the sound *hiṅ*.
The risen sun is the Introductory Chant.
The midday sun is the High Chant.
The afternoon sun is the Response Chant.
The setting sun is the Concluding Chant.
This is the *Bṛhad* Sama Chant, which is woven on the movements of the sun.

2. One who knows this *Bṛhad* Sama Chant becomes an eater of food and has a complete and long life, full of offspring, livestock and fame. But he must never complain when it is hot. That is the rule.

Here ends the Fourteenth *Khaṇḍa*

Fifteenth *Khaṇḍa*

The *Vairūpa Sama* Chant

1. Rising mist is the sound *hiṅ*.
Forming clouds are the Introductory Chant.
Rains are the High Chant.
Diminishing rains are the Response Chant.
Finished rains are the Concluding Chant.
This is the *Vairūpa* Sama Chant, which is woven on the progress of rains.

2. One who knows this *Vairūpa* Sama Chant comes to possess wonderful animals of different breeds. He becomes an eater of food and has a complete and long life, full of offspring, livestock and fame. But he must never complain when it rains. That is the rule.

Here ends the Fifteenth *Khaṇḍa*

Sixteenth *Khaṇḍa*

The *Virāja* Sama Chant

1. The spring is the sound *hiṅ*.
The hot season is the Introductory Chant.
The rainy season is the High Chant.
Autumn is the Response Chant.
Winter is the Concluding Chant.
This is the *Virāja* Sama Chant, which is woven on the progress of the seasons.

2. One who knows this *Virāja* Sama Chant becomes replete with children, animals and spiritual power. He has a complete and long life, full of offspring, livestock and fame. But he must never complain against the seasons. That is the rule.

Here ends the Sixteenth *Khaṇḍa*

Seventeenth *Khaṇḍa*

The *Śakvarī* Sama Chant

1. The earth is the sound *hiṅ*.

The sky is the Introductory Chant.
Heaven is the High Chant.
The directions are the Response Chant.
The oceans are the Concluding Chant.
This is the *Śakvarī* Sama Chant, which is woven on the worlds.

2. One who knows this *Śakvarī* Sama Chant comes to own the worlds. He has a complete and long life, full of offspring, livestock and fame. But he must never complain against the worlds. That is the rule.

Here ends the Seventeenth *Khaṇḍa*

Eighteenth *Khaṇḍa*

The *Revatī* Sama Chant

1. Goats are the sound *hiṅ*.
Sheep are the Introductory Chant.
Cows are the High Chant.
Horses are the Response Chant.
Mankind is the Concluding Chant.
This is the *Revatī* Sama Chant, which is woven on animals.

2. One who knows this *Revatī* Sama Chant becomes a possessor of animals. He has a complete and long life, full of offspring, livestock and fame. But he must never complain against animals. That is the rule.

Here ends the Eighteenth *Khaṇḍa*

Nineteenth ***Khaṇḍa***

The *Yajñāyajñīya* Sama Chant

1. Hair is the sound *hiṅ*.
Skin is the Introductory Chant.
Flesh is the High Chant.
Bone is the Response Chant.
Marrow is the Concluding Chant.
This is the *Yajñāyajñīya* Sama Chant, which is woven on the parts of the body.

2. One who knows this *Yajñāyajñīya* Sama Chant becomes a possessor of the body without defects. He has a complete and long life, full of offspring, livestock and fame. But for a year he must not eat marrow. That is the rule. Better still, he should never eat marrow at all.

Here ends the Nineteenth *Khaṇḍa*

Twentieth ***Khaṇḍa***

The *Rājana* Sama Chant

1. Fire is the sound *hiṅ*.
Wind is the Introductory Chant.
Sun is the High Chant.

---

[14] Here the Sanskrit is *salokatā*, *sārṣṭitā* and *sāyujya*, the same worlds, the same rank and the same likeness respectively.

The lunar mansions are the Response Chant.
The moon is the Concluding Chant.
This is the *Rājana* Sama Chant, which is woven on the gods.

2. One who knows this *Rājana* Sama Chant obtains the same residence, rank, and form[14] as these gods. He has a complete and long life, full of offspring, livestock and fame. But he must never complain against *brāhmaṇas*. That is the rule.

Here ends the Twentieth *Khaṇḍa*

Twenty-first *Khaṇḍa*

The Sama Chant Built on the Whole

1. The three Vedas are the sound *hiṅ*.
The three worlds are the Introductory Chant.
Fire, wind and sun are the High Chant.
Stars, birds and light rays are the Response Chant.
Snakes, *Gandharvas* and ancestors are the Concluding Chant.
This is the Sama Chant, which is woven on the whole.

2-3. One who knows this Sama Chant becomes the whole. In this regard there is the following verse:

There is nothing better, there is nothing higher
Than these three sets of five.
One who knows this knows the whole.
Indeed, the directions bring him all honors.

In this way, he should revere the Sama Chant with the thought "I am the whole."
This is the rule. Indeed, this is the rule!

Here ends the Twenty-first *Khaṇḍa*

Twenty-second *Khaṇḍa*

The Ways of Chanting

1. I choose the thundering way of chanting Sama. It resembles the bellowing of a bull and it is the High Chant of Agni. The softer way is the Chant of Prajapati. A medium way is the Chant of Soma. The still more soft and gentle way is the Chant of Vayu. The smooth and strong way is of Indra, and the way of the crane is the Chant of Brihaspati. The dissident way is of Varuna and should never be used. All these other ways of chanting may be used.

2. One should chant with all care while thinking "Let my chanting obtain immortality for the gods, oblations for the ancestors, hope for mankind, grass and water for livestock, heaven for the

---

[15] Here the word *atyantam* is used. It means "until the very end," i.e., death. In the old system of education, a Vedic student would take a vow of *brahmacarya* and so became a *brahmacārī:* literally, one who goes in the way of *brahma.* In other words, a seeker of *brahma*. This generally meant taking the vow of celibacy There were two kinds of *brahmacārīs:* the most common form, the *upakurvāna,* who would leave the house of the teacher after graduation and get married; and the *naiṣṭhakī,* who would not marry and remain until death at the house of the teacher. Both forms were considered pious.

patron of the sacrifice, and food for myself."

3. Vowels are the body of Indra, sibilants are the body of Prajapati, and consonants are the body of Death. If someone should, therefore, criticize your chanting of the vowels, say to him, "I have taken shelter of Indra, so now you will have to answer to Indra himself."

4. If someone should criticize your chanting of the sibilants, let them know you have taken shelter of Prajapati, and so Prajapati himself will crush them. If someone should criticize your chanting of the consonants, tell them you have taken shelter of Death, and so Death himself will scorch him.

5. Vowels should always be chanted with resonance and strength while thinking "I give strength to Indra." Sibilants should be chanted open and full and without shortening while thinking "I give myself to Prajapati." The consonants should be pronounced clearly and distinctly while thinking "I defend myself from death."

Here ends the Twenty-second *Khaṇḍa*

Twenty-third *Khaṇḍa*

The Three Pillars of Dharma

1. Dharma is comprised of three pillars. Sacrifice, study and charity are the first pillar. Austerity is the second pillar, and adopting a vow of celibacy and residing at the home of the teacher is the third pillar.[15] All these lead to the worlds of the

pious. Indeed, one fixed in *brahma* attains immortality.

2. Prajapati cooked these worlds and from his cooking the three Vedas boiled up. He then cooked the three Vedas and the syllables *bhūr*, *bhuvas* and *svar* boiled up. He finally cooked these three syllables and the single syllable *om* boiled up. As leaves are bound together on the same stem, so all speech is bound by the syllable *om*. Indeed, this whole world is bound together by *Om*!

Here ends the Twenty-third *Khaṇḍa*

---

[16] In other words, there must be a tangible reward for the *yajamāna*.

[17] The *Gārhapatya fire,* or the householder's fire, is one of three main fires used in the Vedic sacrifice. It is located on the western side of the sacrificial enclosure.

[18] This verse, which is repeated, with slight variation, four times in this chapter, is an excellent example of vowel lengthening (prolation). It is a rare thing to see, so here is what the transliterated Sanskrit looks like. The numerals indicate the length of prolation or vowel lengthening, 1 being one measure long, 2 being two measures, and 3 being three measures.
lo 3 *ka-dvāram apāvā* 3 *rṇū* 3 3/ *paśyema tvā vayaṃ rā* 3 3 3 3 3
hu 3 m ā 3 3 *jyā* 3 yo 3 *ā* 3 2 1 1 1

[19] The *Agnīdhrīya* fire another of the three main fires, is connected to the *āgnīdhra* priest, who is an assistant priest responsible for maintaining the fires.

Twenty-fourth *Khaṇḍa*

The Rewards of Sacrifice

1-2. Those who speak of *brahma* ask the following: If the morning pressing of *soma* is for the *Vasus*, and the midday pressing is for the *Rudras*, and the third pressing is for the *Adityas* and *Vishvadevas*, what world is left for the performer of a sacrifice, the *yajamāna*? Without knowing the answer, why would anyone perform a sacrifice?[16] Therefore, only one who knows the answer should perform sacrifice.

3. Facing the north from behind the *Gārhapatya* fire[17] and just before the morning recitations are to commence, the *yajamāna* should sing the following Sama Chant to the Vasus:

4. Open the door to your world
That I might see you
And win sovereignty![18]

5-6. He then makes an oblation, saying "Adorations to Agni, the fire, who lives on the earth. Adorations to Fire, who dwells in this world. Find a world for me, this sacrificer, so I might reach this place. After death this sacrificer will go there. Push back the bolt that I might enter this realm." So saying, he stands and the Vasus present him with the morning pressing of *soma*.

7. Facing north behind the *Agnīdhrīya* fire[19] and just before the midday recitations are to commence, the *yajamāna* should sing

the following Sama Chant to the Rudras:

8. Open the door to your world
That I might see you
And win even greater sovereignty!

9-10. He then makes an oblation saying, "Adorations to Vayu, the wind, who lives in the sky. Adorations to Vaju, who dwells in this world. Find a world for me, this sacrificer, so I might reach this place. After death this sacrificer will go there. Push back the bolt that I might enter this realm." So saying, he stands and the Rudras present him with the midday pressing of *soma*.

11. Facing north behind the *Āhavanīya* fire[20] and just before the third recitations are to commence, the y*ajamāna* should sing the following Sama Chants to the Adityas and the Viśvadevas:

12. Open the door to your world
That I might see you
And win even more sovereignty!

This was the chant for the Adityas.

13. Here is the chant for the Vishvadevas:

[20] The *Āhavanīya* fire is also one of the three main fires. This fire is situated on the eastern side of the sacrificial arena.

Open the door to your world
That I might see you
And win full sovereignty!

14-15. He then makes an oblation, saying, "Adorations to the Adityas and the Vishvadevas' who live in the heavens. Adorations to the Adityas and the Vishvadevas who live in this world. Find a world for me, this sacrificer, so I might reach this place. After death this sacrificer will go there. Push back the bolt that I might enter this realm."

16. So saying, he stands and the Adityas and the Vishvadevas present him with the third pressing of Soma. He who knows these things knows the full extent of the sacrifice. Indeed, he knows!

Here ends the Twenty-fourth *Khaṇḍa*

Here ends the Second *Adhyāya*

Third *Adhyāya*

First *Khaṇḍa*

Honey of the Rig

1. The sun on high is honey for the gods. Heaven is the beehive. The regions beyond the heavens are the honeycombs, and the glittering stars are the larvae.

2. The sun's eastern rays are the easterly honey cells. The Rig verses are the bees, the makers of honey, and the Rig itself is the flower, the very nectar of life.

3. These verses, having simmered in the Rig, gave rise to beauty, luster, power, strength and food. All this flowed toward the sun, from which its color has become red.

Here ends the First *Khaṇḍa*

Second *Khaṇḍa*

Honey of the Yajur

1. The sun's southern rays are the southern honey cells. The Yajur verses are the bees, the makers of honey, and the Yajur itself is the flower, the very nectar of life.

2-3. These verses, having simmered in the Yajur, gave rise to beauty, luster, power, strength and food. All this flowed to the sun, from which its color has become white.

Here ends the Second *Khaṇḍa*

Third *Khaṇḍa*

Honey of the Sama

1. The sun's western rays are the western honey cells. The Sama verses are the bees, the makers of honey, and the Sama itself is the flower, the very nectar of life.

2-3. These verses, having simmered in the Sama, gave rise to beauty, luster, power, strength and food. All this flowed to the sun, from which its color has become dark.

Here ends the Third *Khaṇḍa*

---

[1] Here the Sanskrit is *arthava-aṅgirasa.* This is the full name for the Arthava Veda.

[2] Here the words for the histories and ancient stories are *itihāsa* and *purāṇa,* respectively. In later Hinduism the Histories are the two epics, the Mahabharata and the Ramayana, and the Ancient Stories have come to mean the numerous Puranic texts such as the Skanda and Matsya Puranas, etc.

[3] The words are *guhyā evādeśāḥ*, hidden teachings. Commentators generally take this as the Upanishads, but another meaning "substitution" may also apply. See BU 2.3.6 fn.

[4] Here *brahma* may mean the Vedas or even the syllable *om*.

Fourth *Khaṇḍa*

Honey of the *Atharva* Veda

1. The sun's northern rays are the northern honey cells. The Atharva[1] verses are the bees, the makers of honey, and the histories and ancient stories[2] are the flowers, the very nectar of life.

2-3. This Atharva, having simmered in the histories and ancient stories, gave rise to beauty, luster, power, strength and food. All this flowed to the sun, from which its color has become black.

Here ends the Fourth *Khaṇḍa*

Fifth *Khaṇḍa*

The Vedas as the Essence

1. The upward rays of the sun are the upper honey cells. The bees are the hidden teachings,[3] the Upanishads, and *brahma*[4] is the flower. These waters are the nectar.

2-3. These hidden teachings, being cooked and simmered in the Vedas, have produced many wonderful things: beauty, luster, power, strength and food. All this has flowed to the sun, which is why there is a slight quivering at the center of the sun.

4. These are the Vedas, the essence of all things, the immortal nectar of all nectar.[5]

Here ends the Fifth *Khaṇḍa*

Sixth *Khaṇḍa*

The First Nectar

1-2. The Vasus live on the first nectar, the Rig, and have Agni as their mouth. These gods neither eat nor drink their food. Instead, they become satiated simply by seeing. They enter into that red form of the sun and then emerge from that form.

3. One who understands this nectar becomes one of the Vasus and, having Agni as his mouth, eats and becomes satiated simply by seeing. He too enters into the same reddish form of the sun and then again emerges from that same form.

4. So long as the sun rises in the east and sets in the west this person will have the same lordship and sovereignty as the Vasus.

Here ends the Sixth *Khaṇḍa*

---

[5] The actual wording of this section is much more complex than what is shown above. A more literal reading would be "These are the essences of essences. The Vedas are the essences. These are the essences of them. They are the nectar of nectars. The Vedas are the nectars. These are the nectars of them."

[6] This reference is obscure.

Seventh *Khaṇḍa*

The Second Nectar

1-2. The Rudras live on the second nectar, the Yajur, and have Indra as their mouth. These gods neither eat nor drink their food. Instead, they become satiated simply by seeing. They enter into that white form of the sun and then emerge from that form.

3. One who understands this nectar becomes one of the Rudras and, having Indra as his mouth, eats and becomes satiated simply by seeing. He too enters into the same whitish form of the sun and then again emerges from that same form.

4. For as long as the sun rises in the south and sets in the north,[6] which is twice as long as the sun rises in the east and sets in the west, this person will have the same lordship and sovereignty as the Rudras.

Here ends the Seventh *Khaṇḍa*

Eighth *Khaṇḍa*

The Third Nectar

1-2. Next, the Adityas live on the third nectar, the Sama, and have Varuna as their mouth. These gods neither eat nor drink their food. Instead, they become satiated simply by seeing. They enter into that dark form of the sun and then emerge from that form.

3. One who understands this nectar becomes one of the Adityas and, having Varuna as his mouth, eats and becomes satiated simply by seeing. He too enters into the same dark form of the sun and then again emerges from that form.

4. For as long as the sun rises in the west and sets in the east,[7] which is twice as long as the sun rises in the south and sets in the north, this person will have the same lordship and sovereignty as the Adityas.

Here ends the Eighth *Khaṇḍa*

Ninth *Khaṇḍa*

The Fourth Nectar

1-2. Next, the Maruts live on the fourth nectar, the Atharva, and have Soma as their mouth. These gods neither eat nor drink their food. Instead, they become satiated simply by seeing. They enter into that black form of the sun and then emerge from that form.

3. One who understands this nectar becomes one of the Maruts and, having Soma as his mouth, eats and becomes satiated simply by seeing. He too enters into the same black form of the sun and then again emerges from that form.

---

[7] Again, this reference is obscure.

[8] This is being referenced from CU 3.5.1, where the word was *ādeśa,* which had a basic meaning of just "teachings."

4. For as long as the sun rises in the north and sets in the south, which is twice as long as the sun rises in the west and sets in the east, this person will have the same lordship and sovereignty as the Maruts.

Here ends the Ninth *Khaṇḍa*

Tenth *Khaṇḍa*

The Fifth Nectar

1-2. Next, the Sadhyas live on the fifth nectar, the Upanishads,[8] and have Brahmā as their mouth. These gods neither eat nor drink their food. Instead, they become satiated simply by seeing. They enter into that form, which seems to quiver at the middle of the sun, and then emerge from that same form.

3. One who understands this fifth nectar becomes one of the Sadhyas and, having Brahmā as his mouth, eats and becomes satiated simply by seeing. He too enters into the same form, which seems to quiver at the middle of the sun, and then again emerges from that same form.

4. For as long as the sun rises at the zenith and sets at the nadir, which is twice as long as the sun rises in the north and sets in the south, this person will have the same lordship and sovereignty as the Sadhyas.

Here ends the Tenth *Khaṇḍa*

Eleventh *Khaṇḍa*

Where the Sun Never Rises or Sets

1-2. Thereupon having reached its zenith, the sun will never again rise or set. It will remain fixed, solitary and overhead. In this regard there is the following verse:

In this realm there is never any rising or setting of the sun.
O ye gods, never let me be deprived of this truth of *brahma*.

3. For one who knows this mystical doctrine of *brahma* the sun never rises or sets. For that person it is always daytime.

---

[9] This is the first unambiguous mention of the creator god, Brahmā.

[10] The word is *bhūta*, which means all things which have come into existence. This includes both animate and inanimate things.

[11] The word for speech is *vāc*, which means language. When the text says "speech sings of all things," it means language names and defines all things. Here the word *gāyatrī* is composed of two roots, *gai* and *trai*. *Gai* means to sing and *trai* means to protect, and so through language all things are articulated and thereby defined.

[12] Here the word is *prāṇa*, which has three basic meanings: breath, the senses, and the vital functions, such as circulation, digestion, elimination, etc.

Eleventh *Khaṇḍa*

4-6. In the past Brahmā[9] spoke this secret doctrine to Prajapati, who in turn spoke it to Manu. Manu then spoke it to his descendants. And his father spoke this knowledge to his eldest son, Uddalaka Aruṇi. Indeed, a father should reveal this sacred learning to his eldest son or most cherished disciple, but not to others. Even if he is offered this whole earth surrounded by water and filled with wealth, he should think, "This knowledge is worth more than this; indeed, much more than this!"

Here ends the Eleventh *Khaṇḍa*

Twelfth *Khaṇḍa*

Gāyatrī

1. Whatever exists in the world[10] is defined by *gāyatrī*. Speech is *gāyatrī*. Speech sings of all things and protects all things.[11]

2. The earth itself is *gāyatrī*. All that exists is bound by this earth and so all things here never extend beyond the earth.

3. What the earth is to the universe the body is for a man. All the senses[12] are rooted in this body and so they never extend beyond the body.

4. What the body is to a man the heart is for the body. All the vital functions are rooted within the heart and so they never extend beyond the heart.

[13] This *gāyatrī* is said to have four feet or *padas*. The word for foot is *pada*, and as an animal stands on four feet, so *gāyatrī* has four feet. A *pada* is also a quarter and one line of poetry. A typical stanza of Sanskrit poetry will have four lines or *padas*. This is what is meant by four feet. Here *gāyatrī* is also said to be sixfold. In this case it refers to the six constituents mentioned in this chapter, *bhūta*, *vāc*, *pṛthivī*, *śarīra*, *prāṇa* and *hṛdaya, i.e.,* the animate and inanimate objects, speech, earth, breath, body, and heart.

[14] This is a variation of Rig 10.90.3, the famous *Puruṣa-sukta*. According to this *sukta,* a cosmic form of *brahma* called *puruṣa,* which literally means man, is offered as a sacrifice to create this world. The eye of this cosmic "man" becomes the sun, his mind becomes the moon, his breathing the wind, etc.

[15] The notion that there is an equivalence between the outside world and the inside world, and even between the part and its whole, is a common theme throughout the Upanishads.

[16] The word is *śrī,* and, in addition to wealth, it means splendor, beauty and majesty.

[17] See BU 1.3 fn 5 for more information on *prāṇa*. *Prāṇa* is the general word for breath, but there are also five derivative breaths, sometimes called *vayus* or winds. These five derivative breaths are listed here in verses 1-5. Although the meanings of these breaths have evolved over time and even vary from Upanishad to Upanishad in general p*rāṇa* is the in-breath, *apāna* is the out-breath, *vyāna* is the held breath*, samāna* is the "breath" of digestion responsible for evacuation, etc., and *udāna* is the "up-breath," the breath responsible for burping and vomiting, etc.

[18] The word here is *cakṣus*, which can be the eye or sight. The same applies to the next verse that mentions ear. It could be translated as hearing.

[19] Literally, an eater of food.

5-6. This *gāyatrī* has four feet and is sixfold.[13] This has been mentioned in the following Rig verse:[14]

Such is the greatness of this *puruṣa*,
But greater still is He.
His one quarter are all beings in this world,
His three quarters are the immortals in heaven.

7-9. What people call *brahma* is the space outside a person. This space outside a person is the same as the space within a person. And the space within a person is the same as the space within the heart.[15] It is immovable and complete. One who understands this obtains complete and constant wealth.[16]

Here ends the Twelfth *Khaṇḍa*

Thirteenth *Khaṇḍa*

Five Pathways of the Heart

1. The heart has five divine pathways. On the east there is *prāṇa*.[17] It is the eye.[18] It is the sun. One who honors this pathway as the source of splendor and nourishment becomes himself full of splendor and nourishment.[19]

2. On the south there is *vyāna*. It is the ear. It is the moon. One who honors this pathway as the source of beauty and fame becomes himself endowed with beauty and fame.

3. On the west there is *apāna*. It is speech. It is fire. One who

honors this pathway as the source of spiritual opulence[20] and nourishment becomes himself endowed with spiritual opulence and nourishment.

4. On the north there is *samāna*. It is the mind. It is rain. One who honors this pathway as the source of renown and grace becomes himself endowed with renown and grace.

5. On the upper direction there is *udāna*. It is wind. It is space. One who honors this pathway as the source of vigor and might becomes himself endowed with vigor and might.

---

[20] *Brahma-varchasa*, literally the luster of *brahma.*

[21] In other words, as something real and tangible.

[22] That is to say, seen and heard.

[23] "S*arvaṃ khalv idaṃ brahma.*" This is one of the numerous *mahā-vakyas*, defining statements, of the Upanishads.

[24] Here the Sanskrit reads *tajjalān.* This expression is obscure. Some commentators say it is a hapax, or single usage code, for *tat-ja-la-an: tat* being the neuter pronoun "that," meaning *brahma*, "*ja*" meaning birth, "*la*" meaning destruction, and "*an*" meaning to breath or to live. Hence, the translation "All things arise from *brahma*, all things are maintained in *brahma*, all things dissolve into *brahma*." Others say it is a corrupted form of "*tat jānāni,*" "I know that *brahma*."

[25] Here the expression is *kratu-maya*, "made" or "full of *kratu.*" *Kratu* has the following shades of meaning: will, power, determination, resolve, intention. This sentence could just as easily be translated as "all beings are comprised of will."

[26] "Manifests in physical reality" is a gloss on *ākāśātmā, ākāśa* being space and *ātmā* being the body.

6. These five "*brahma*-men" are the gatekeepers of heaven, and for one who knows this, a hero will be born into his family and he will ascend to heaven. Indeed, he will ascend to heaven!

7-8. That light which shines down from far above to all places and on the backs of all things, and even in the highest of heavens, is the same light which shines inside a man. It is perceived when one touches the body and feels the warmth within. It is heard when the ears are held shut and one hears the sound within like a roaring fire. One should honor this light as something seen and heard.[21] One who truly knows this will become himself handsome and famous.[22]

Here ends the Thirteenth *Khaṇḍa*

Fourteenth *Khaṇḍa*

The Knowledge of *Shandilya*

1. "All this indeed is *brahma.*[23] All things arise from *brahma*, all things are maintained in *brahma*, and all things dissolve into *brahma*!"[24] Free of passion, take shelter of this knowledge. All beings are driven by desire.[25] As they desire in this world so they become in the next world. Reflect on the following:

2. This *ātmā,* laying deep within my heart, manifests in physical reality[26] as this luminous body, full of mind and senses, seeking truth, full of actions and desires, fragrances and tastes. It embraces this world silently and without concern.

3. This *ātmā*, lying deep within my heart, is smaller than a grain of rice, a seed of mustard or a kernel of millet. This *ātmā*, lying deep within my heart, is larger than the earth, larger than the sky, and even the heavens. It is greater than all these worlds combined.

4. Full of actions and desires, fragrances and tastes, this *ātmā* embraces this world silently and without concern. Lying deep within my heart, it is *brahma.* Departing this world I will become *brahma*. Of this there is no doubt. This is the knowledge of Shandilya! Yea, this is the knowledge of Shandilya![27]

Here ends the Fourteenth *Khaṇḍa*

---

[27] He is one of the important teachers of the *agni hotra* in the SB, to whom is ascribed a famous doctrine bearing his name, "Sandilya-doctrine" (*sandilya-vidya*), in SB 10.6.3 and CU 3.14.

[28] These are the names of the four directions. According to *vāstu-śastra*, the ancient Indian system of architecture, east is the direction of Indra. It is the direction of *yajña*, sacrifice, and one faces this direction during a sacrifice. South is the direction of Yama, the god of death, and so one faces this direction during funerary rites. West is the direction of King Varuna, and so it is called *rajñī*, the queen. North is the direction of Kuvera, the treasurer of the gods, and so it is the direction of prosperity. And so one constructing a home, for example, would put the "money room" on the northern side.

[29] Literally the Sanskrit says *amunā amunā amunā*, "with him, with him, with him." This suggests one should repeat the son's name three times during this prayer.

[30] *Bhūr, bhuvas* and *svar* are the three *vyahṛtis* or mystical utterances, recited during prayers and rituals. See TU 1.5.1

Fifteenth *Khaṇḍa*

The Treasure Chest

1. There is a treasure chest that never decays.
Its inside is the sky.
Its bottom is the earth.
Its corners are the directions, and it opens to the heavens.
This treasure chest contains all wealth and it supports all things.

2. Its eastern side is called *juhū*. It is a sacrificial ladle. Its southern side is called *sahamānā*, "conquering," because death conquers all things. Its western side is called *rājñī*, the queen, and its northern side is called *subhūta*, prosperous.[28]

Vāyu, the wind, is the child of these directions. Anyone who knows this will never mourn the loss of a son. I know this, so let me not mourn the loss of a son!

3. Along with my son[29] I take shelter in this treasure chest.
Along with my son I take shelter in breath.
Along with my son I take shelter in *bhūr*.
Along with my son I take shelter in *bhuvas*.
Along with my son I take shelter in *svar*.[30]

4. Whatever there is in this world is founded on breath. So when I said, "I take shelter in breath," it was to this breath that I sought shelter.

5. When I said, "I take shelter in *bhūr*," I meant, "I take shelter of the earth, I take shelter of the sky, I take shelter of the heavens."

6. When I said, "I take shelter in *bhuvas*," I meant, "I take shelter of fire, I take shelter of wind, I take shelter of the sun."

7. When I said, "I take shelter in *svar*," I meant, "I take shelter of the Rig, I take shelter of the Yajur, I take shelter of the Sama."

Here ends the Fifteenth *Khaṇḍa*

Sixteenth *Khaṇḍa*

The Doctrine of 116

1-2. A man is a sacrifice. His first twenty-four years are the morning pressing of *soma*. *Gāyatrī* meter consists of twenty-four syllables,[31] so the morning pressing of *soma* is done with

---

[31] *Gāyatrī* is a meter of three lines of eight syllables.

[32] There are eight Vasus, and so the association with the *gāyatrī* meter.

[33] The verb is *vāsayanti* from the root *vas*, to reside. In other words, all beings reside in this world due to breath.

[34] *Triṣṭubh* is a meter of four lines of eleven syllables.

[35] There are eleven Rudras, and so the association with the *triṣṭubh* meter.

[36] *Jagatī* is a meter of four lines of twelve syllables.

[37] There are twelve Adityas, and so the association with the *jagatī* meter.

gāyatrī. The Vasus[32] are the breaths that govern this part of the sacrifice. Because of these breaths this whole universe is maintained.[33] At this stage of life, if one should be afflicted with disease, let him pray, "O breaths, O Vasus, let this morning pressing of *soma* extend into the midday pressing. May I, the sacrifice, not perish during the time of these breaths and these Vasus!" One who does this will become free of disease.

3-4. His next forty-four years are the midday pressing of *soma*. *Triṣṭubh* meter consists of forty-four syllables,[34] so the midday pressing of *soma* is done with *triṣṭubh*. The Rudras[35] are the breaths that govern this part of the sacrifice. This whole universe weeps due to these breaths. At this stage of life, if one should be afflicted with disease, let him pray, "O breaths, O Rudras, let this midday pressing of *soma* extend into the third pressing. May I, the sacrifice, not perish during the time of these breaths and these Rudras!" One who does this will become free of disease.

5-6. And, finally, the next forty-eight years are the third pressing of *soma*. The *jagatī* meter consists of forty-eight syllables[36], so the third pressing of *soma* is done with *jagatī*. The Adityas[37] are the breaths that govern this part of the sacrifice. This whole universe is taken back due to these breaths. At this stage of life, if one should be afflicted with disease, let him pray, "O breaths, O Adityas, let this third pressing of *soma* extend until the end of my life. May I, the sacrifice, not perish during the time of these breaths and these Adityas!" One who does this will become free of disease.

7. Indeed, the learned Mahidasa Aitareya has said, "Why do you afflict me with this disease? I will not die from it." Mahidasa lived to be one hundred and sixteen years. One who understands this will also live to be a hundred and sixteen years.[38]

Here Ends the Sixteenth *Khaṇḍa*

---

[38] It appears the natural span of life was one hundred and sixteen years.

[39] Following the theme of the previous chapter—that a man is a sacrifice—this chapter (verses 1-5) compares the life of a man, from birth to death, with the main elements of the *soma* sacrifice, the initiation *(dikṣā)*, the various rites (*upasad)*, the chants and recitations (*stuta-śastra)*, gifts to the priests (*dakṣinā)*, the regeneration (*punar-utpādana),* and the final ritual bath (*avabhṛtha)*. The initiatory rites in the soma sacrifice, such as penance and fasting, for example, are compared to the afflictions of life. The experience of pain is common to both.

[40] Here the full and literal meaning is "He will press (*soṣyati*) and he has pressed (*asoṣṭa*)." But there is another implied meaning because the verb could be either *su* or *sū.* The first means to press or extract. The second means to procreate. It is no coincidence that these two verbs are used. The extraction of the soma juice, the very essence of the sacrifice, is compared to the rebirth or rejuvenation of man.

[41] Commentators generally agree this is not the famous Kṛṣṇa of the Mahabharata.

[42] Here the "You" is *brahma.*

[43] Here only the first line of Rig 8.6.30 is shown. To make sense of this, the following two lines need to be supplied, *jyotiḥ paśyanti vāsaram/ paro yad idhyate divā.*

[44] This is a variation of Rig 1.50.10

Seventeenth *Khaṇḍa*

The Life of Man is a Sacrifice

1-5 When a man hungers, when he thirsts, and when he has no enjoyment, this is his initiation *(dikṣā).*[39] When he eats, drinks, and enjoys, these are the various rites (*upasad*). When he laughs, feasts, and makes love, these are the chants and recitations (*stuta-śastra*). His austerity, charity, straightforwardness, non-violence, and speaking of the truth, are his gifts to the priests *(dakṣinā)*. And when they say, "He has pressed *soma*,"[40] this is his regeneration (*punar-utpādana*). And at the end, his sacrificial bath *(avabhṛtha)* is his death.

6. When he spoke these teachings to Krishna, the son of Devaki,[41] Ghora Angirasa also said, "In the final moments before death, becoming free of desire, one should think three thoughts: You are imperishable; You are infallible; You are the very essence of life."[42] In this regard there are two Rig verses:

7. Flowing from this ancient seed they see that morning light which shines from beyond the highest heaven.[43]

Seeing beyond all darkness, we see that higher light, we see that higher heaven. We have reached the sun, that god of gods. We have reached that highest light; yea, we have reached that highest light![44]

Here ends the Seventeenth *Khaṇḍa*

Eighteenth *Khaṇḍa*

Brahma in Both the Individual and the Universe

1. In relation to the body,[45] the mind should be respected as *brahma*. In relation to the heavens,[46] space[47] should be respected as *brahma*. This is the correspondence between the bodily realm and the heavenly realm.[48]

2. *Brahma* has four pillars:[49] speech, breath, sight and hearing. These are all in relation to the bodily realm. Similarly, in the heavenly realm *brahma* has four pillars: fire, wind, sun and the directions. This too is the correspondence between the bodily realm and the heavenly realm.

---

[45] Here the word is *adhyātmā.* In this context *ātmā* refers to the body. The prefix *adhi* has the sense of "in relation to."

[46] Here the word is *adhidaiva. Ibid.* fn 1. *Daiva* is derived from *deva*, "god."

[47] Here the word is *ākāsa.*

[48] The correspondence between the bodily world and the heavenly world–between the world "down here" and the world "up there"–is a recurrent theme throughout the Upanishads.

[49] Here the word is *pada*, which literally means a foot. However, it also means a quarter. See RV 10.90.3.

[50] The words used here are *asat* and *sat*, non-being and being. One possible reading of this sentence is "In the beginning there was non-being, and from non-being being arose." Later on in this Upanishad (6.2), this view, that being arose from non-being, is refuted.

3. Speech is one of the four pillars of *brahma*. It shines and glows using fire as its light. One who knows this also shines and glows with fame, glory and the luster of *brahma*.

4. Breath is one of the four pillars of *brahma*. It shines and glows using wind as its light. One who knows this also shines and glows with fame, glory and the luster of *brahma*.

5. Sight is one of the four pillars of *brahma*. It shines and glows using the sun as its light. One who knows this also shines and glows with fame, glory and the luster of *brahma*.

6. Hearing is one of the four pillars of *brahma*. It shines and glows using the directions as its light. One who knows this also shines and glows with fame, glory and the luster of *brahma*.

Here ends the Eighteenth *Khaṇḍa*

Nineteenth *Khaṇḍa*

The Sun as *Brahma*

1. The sun is *brahma*. This is the teaching. Now here is the explanation.

In the beginning there was nothing; then existence arose.[50] As it developed an egg formed. This egg incubated for a year and finally split into two, one half silver and the other half gold.

2. The silver half became the earth and the gold half became the heavens. The outer membrane of this egg became the mountains; the inner membrane became the clouds and mist. Its veins became the rivers, and its embryonic fluid became the oceans.

3. The sun, which we see in the sky, soon appeared, and, as it did, cries of joy and adulation rose up from all beings along with their hopes and dreams. Each time the sun rises and sets we therefore hear the cries of joy and adulation from all beings.

4. One who understands this relationship between the sun and *brahma* can expect the sounds of joy and adulation to reach him. Indeed, he rejoices!

Here Ends the Nineteenth *Khaṇḍa*
Here Ends the Third Adhyāya

Fourth *Adhyāya*

First *Khaṇḍa*

Raikva, The Man with the Cart

1. There was once a faithful man, the grandson of Janashruti, who was charitable and devoted to the giving of food. He had constructed many rest houses throughout the land, so he used to think, "People can now eat my food everywhere."

2. One evening wild geese were flying by and one said to the other, "Hey, Bright-Eyes, see that light in the sky? It's from Janashruti. Don't let it touch you lest you get burned."

3. The other replied, "Oh, come now, why do you speak of him as if he were another Raikva, the man with the cart? How is he at all like that Raikva?"

4. The first of the geese replied, "As in a game of dice, where all the lower throws go to the winning throw, so whatever good things people do all go to him. I say the same of anyone who knows what Raikva knows."

5-6. Janashruti heard this conversation and, on getting up in the morning, said to his attendant, "Sir! This is what I heard: 'Oh, come now, why do you speak of him as if he were another Raikva, the man with the cart? How is he at all like that Raikva?' 'As in a game of dice where all the lower throws go to the winning throw, so whatever good things people do all go to him. I say the same of anyone who knows what Raikva knows.'"

7. Immediately the attendant went searching for Raikva, but could not find him, and so he returned. Janashruti then told him to search in a place where non-*brāhmanas* can be found.[1]

8. Eventually the attendant found a man living under a cart who was scratching his sores. He asked him, "Are you Raikva, the man with the cart?"

The man replied, "Yes, it's me!"

The attendant returned, saying, "I have found him, sir."

Here Ends the First *Khaṇḍa*

---

[1] There are two possible readings of the text, *brāhamaṇasyānveṣaṇā* or *abrāhamaṇasyānveṣaṇā*, "search in the place of *brāhmaṇas*" or "search in the place of non- *brāhmaṇas*."

[2] The word is literally *mahā-vṛṣa*, great bull. Presumably because this area was started with so many cows as a result of Janashruti's donation, his descendants got this name.

Second *Khaṇḍa*

Janashruti Approaches Raikva

1-2. Janashruti then assembled a collection of six hundred cows, gold ornaments, and carriages pulled by she-mules. He then went to Raikva and spoke: "Good sir, I bring you six hundred cows, gold ornaments, and carriages pulled by she-mules! Pray, teach me which god you worship."

3-4. But Raikva rebuked him saying, "You *sūdra*! Take your cows and gold back home."

Janashruti then assembled a collection of one thousand cows, more gold, and more carriages pulled by she-mules, and even his own daughter. Again he went to Raikva and spoke: "Good sir, I bring you one thousand cows, more gold ornaments, and carriages pulled by she-mules, and even a wife and your own villages. Pray, teach me which god you worship."

5. Gazing into the face of the girl, Raikva spoke, "*Śūdra*, drive these cows to my place. With just this face alone you could have gotten me to speak!"

And to this day these villages where Janashruti met Raikva are called Raikvaparṇa by the people of the "great bulls."[2]

Here ends the Second *Khaṇḍa*

Third *Khaṇḍa*

Janashruti Speaks with Raikva

1-2. Wind consumes all things. When a fire is extinguished, it is absorbed by wind. When the sun sets, it vanishes into the wind. When the moon sets, it also vanishes into the wind. When water evaporates, it is taken by the wind. Indeed, wind consumes all things.

This is in terms of the heavens.

3. Now in terms of the body:

Breath consumes all things. When a man sleeps, speech merges into breath. Sight, hearing and mind also merge into breath. All these vital functions are consumed by breath.

---

[3] On the celestial level, that one god is the wind, who swallows fire, sun, moon and water. On the bodily level, that one god is breath, who swallows the vital functions, such as speech, sight, hearing and thought. Wind is the breath of the gods.

[4] The ten have been mentioned above: wind, fire, sun, moon, water, breath, speech, sight, hearing and mind. These ten are compared to the highest throw of dice.

[5] Some commentators read the text as *draṣṭa,* "to see." I am reading the text as *daṣṭa,* "to bite."This makes more sense because the whole theme is about food and the eater of food.

4. Wind and breath are the consumers. In the divine realm, wind consumes all; and amongst the bodily functions, breath consumes all.

5. Once, when Shaunaka Kapeya and Abhipratarina Kakshaseni were eating, a Vedic student approached them and asked for food. They refused him.

6. In response the student asked them:

"One god, who is the protector of the world, has swallowed four great gods. Oh, learned men, mortals cannot see this god even though he resides everywhere. Who is that god?[3]

You have not given food to the one who deserves food!"

7. Shaunaka Kapeya considered this and replied,

"He is the soul of the gods, the father of all creatures, the wise devourer of all things with blazing teeth. It is said that his wonder is beyond measure. He eats what is not food, yet no beings eat him. Oh, student, we venerate this One! Give this boy food."

8. They gave him food.

Now these five and those five make ten,[4] the highest throw of dice. Therefore, in all cases ten is the highest throw of dice. It is food alone; it is this shining one who has sunk his teeth[5] into this whole world. And one who knows this also sinks his teeth into this world and becomes an eater of food.[6]

Here ends the Third *Khaṇḍa*

Fourth *Khaṇḍa*

Teachings to Satyakama Jabala

1. Once Satyakama Jabala spoke to his mother. "I wish to become a student.[7] What is my lineage?"[8]

2. His mother replied, "My dear boy, I do not know. In my youth

---

[6] Throughout the Upanishads the theme of food and the eater of food is common.

[7] The word is *brahmacārī*, which literally means "one who goes in the way of *brahma*." In other words, the boy wanted to be admitted as a Vedic student.

[8] The word is *gotra,* and it refers to a paternal family lineage. Admission as a Vedic student often depended on having the right ancestry.

[9] Many traditional commentators say this means that the mother was so busy attending to her domestic duties that she had no time to pay attention to her family ancestry!

[10] In other words, to admit the truth that one's mother was a little loose in her younger days and that one was a bastard is the sign of a true *brāhmaṇa*. Truth is the foundation of being a *brāhmaṇa.*

Fourth *Khaṇḍa*

I used to get around a bit[9] and that is when you were born. So I do not know your lineage. But since my name is Jabala and your name is Satyakama tell your teacher that your name is Satyakama Jabala."

3. He went to the teacher, Haridrumata Gautama, and said, "Sir, I wish to become a student. So I approach you."

4. Haridrumata Gautama asked him, "My dear boy, what is your lineage?"

The boy replied, "Good sir, I asked my mother, but she said she did not know my lineage. She told me, 'In my youth I used to get around a bit and that is when you were born. So I do not know your lineage. But since my name is Jabala and your name is Satyakama tell your teacher that your name is Satyakama Jabala.'"

5. Haridrumata replied, "Who else but a Brahmin would speak like this?[10] Son, fetch the fuel. I will accept you as a student. You have not strayed from the truth!" So he initiated the boy and gave him four hundred weak and skinny cows. As the boy was herding them away, he promised, "I'll not return until they have become a thousand." So he stayed away until the herd grew to a thousand.

Here ends the Fourth *Khaṇḍa*

Fifth *Khaṇḍa*

The Bull Teaches

1-2. Finally, the bull cried out, "Satyakama!"

"Yes sir?" he replied.

"The herd has reached a thousand. Return us to the teacher's home and I'll teach you a quarter of *brahma*."

"Please tell me, sir."

So the bull said, "The east is one part, the west is one part, the south is one part, and the north is one part. My child, these four parts of *brahma* are called 'the shining.'

"One who understands this and so respects this one quarter of *brahma*, himself shines in this world. Such a person wins all the worlds."

Here ends Fifth *Khaṇḍa*

Sixth *Khaṇḍa*

Fire Teaches

1-2. The bull continued, "Fire will teach you the next quarter of

[11] The word is *haṃsa* which generally gets translated as "swan." This is overly elegant as a *haṃsa* is actually a kind of wild goose.

brahma." In the morning Satyakama drove his cows ahead. By the evening he built a fire, corralled his cows, put wood on the fire, and sat facing the east with the fire behind him.

Fire then called to him: "Satyakama."

"Sir?"

"Listen as I teach you the next quarter of *brahma*."

"I am listening, sir."

"The earth is one part, the sky is one part, the heavens are one part, and the oceans are one part. My child, these four parts of *brahma* are called 'limitless.'

3. "One who understands this and so respects this quarter of *brahma,* himself becomes limitless in this world. Such a person wins all these worlds."

Here ends the Sixth *Khaṇḍa*

Seventh *Khaṇḍa*
The Swan Teaches

1-2. Fire continued: "The swan[11] will teach you the next quarter of *brahma*." In the morning Satyakama drove his cows ahead. By the evening he built a fire, corralled his cows, put wood on the fire, and sat facing the east with the fire behind him.

The swan then called to him: "Satyakama."

"Sir?"

"Listen as I teach you the next quarter of *brahma*."

"I am listening, sir."

"Fire is one part, the sun is one part, the moon is one part, and lightning is one part. My child, these four parts of *brahma* are called 'the radiant.'

3. "One who understands this and so respects this quarter of *brahma*, himself becomes radiant in this world. Such a person wins all these worlds."

Here ends the Seventh *Khaṇḍa*

Eighth *Khaṇḍa*

A Water Bird Teaches

1-2. The swan continued: "A water bird will teach you the next quarter of *brahma*."

In the morning Satyakama drove his cows ahead. By the evening he built a fire, corralled his cows, put wood on the fire, and sat facing the east with the fire behind him.

The swan then called to him: "Satyakama."

"Sir?"

"Listen as I teach you the next quarter of *brahma*."

"I am listening, sir."

"Breath is one part, the eye is one part, the ear is one part, and mind is one part. My child, these four parts of *brahma* are called 'the foundation.'

3. "One who understands this and so respects this quarter of *brahma*, himself possesses a foundation in this world. Such a person wins all these worlds."

Here ends the Eighth *Khaṇḍa*

Ninth *Khaṇḍa*

The Teacher Teaches

1. Finally they reached the home of the teacher, Haridrumata. The teacher called to him: "Satyakama!

"Sir?"

2-3. "My son, you are shining like one who knows *brahma*. Who has taught you?"

Satyakama replied, "I have heard from those who are not human. But if it pleases you, sir, teach me; for I have heard that the best knowledge is knowledge learned directly from a respected teacher." So the teacher taught him and nothing was left out. Indeed, nothing was left out!

Tenth *Khaṇḍa*

The Story of Upakosala

1-2. Once upon a time Upakosala Kamalayana lived as a religious student under Satyakama Jabala and for twelve years he tended his teacher's fires. All the other students who were living with their teacher were allowed to return home, but not Upakosala Kamalayana.[12] Finally, Satyakama's wife spoke to her husband: "This student has practiced his vows of penance and he has faithfully tended your fires. Do not allow the fires to speak

---

[12] In other words, they were allowed to graduate.

[13] The word is *prāṇa*. *Prāṇa* is a multifaceted word which can mean breath, the vital senses, or even life itself. Therefore, life is a manifestation of *brahma*.

[14] The word is *kam*, meaning "joy." This suggests emotional life. In the feelings of intense emotion, one experiences *brahma*. This leads to the topic of Hindu aesthetics.

[15] Two words are employed here, *kham* and *ākāśa*, and both have been translated as "space." By "space" is meant the distance between two points. Therefore, wherever one looks, one sees space. This space is *brahma*.

[16] The *gārhapatya* fire is one of the three sacred fires maintained by a householder, which he receives from his father and passes on to his descendants. It is sometimes called the western fire and it is related to *apāna*, one of the five breaths. In a Vedic sacrifice this fire is located to the west of the *vedi*, the sacrificial altar. The patron (*yajamāna*) sits behind, to the west of this fire.

[17] For similar references to seeing a person in the sun see BU 2.3.5; 5.5.2; CU 1.7.5; 8.7.5.

to him before you. Teach him." But Satyakama went traveling abroad before teaching him.

3. Being so afflicted, Upakosala resolved to fast. The wife of the teacher noticed this and said, "Why are you not eating? You must eat!"

4. But Upakosala replied, "All these desires make so many faults within this person. Therefore, I am filled with afflictions and so I will not eat." The fires then talked amongst themselves and said, "This student has practiced his vows well and faithfully tended us; let us teach him." So they taught him, "Breath[13] is *brahma,* joy[14] is *brahma,* and space[15] is *brahma.*"

5. Upakosala replied, "I understand how breath is *brahma*, but I do not understand how joy and space are *brahma*."

The fires answered, "Joy is the same as space and space is the same as joy." They then explained to him breath and space.

Here ends the Tenth *Khaṇḍa*

Eleventh *Khaṇḍa*

Teachings from the Householder's Fire

1. The householder's fire[16] next instructed Upakosala: "Earth, fire, food and sun, these are my forms, and the person you see in the sun, it is I and I alone.[17]

2. "One who understands this becomes released from his misdeeds. Such a person inherits this world and lives a full life with luster. His descendants are never destroyed. In both this world and the next, we protect that person who understands and respects this."

Here ends the Eleventh *Khaṇḍa*

Twelfth *Khaṇḍa*

The Southern Fire Instructs

1. The southern fire[18] next instructed Upakosala: "The waters, the directions, the lunar mansions, and the moon, these are my forms, and the person you see in the moon, it is I and I alone.

2. "One who understands this becomes freed of bad deeds. Such a person inherits this world and lives a full life with luster. His

---

[18] The *anvāhārya-pacana* fire is the southern fire and is connected with *vyāna*, one of the fire "breaths." In a Vedic sacrifice this fire is located to the south of the sacrificial enclosure. It was used for cooking rice. *Pacana* means cooking.

[19] The *āhavanīya* fire is the eastern fire, often related to *prāṇa*, one of the fire "breaths." This fire is located to the east of the sacrificial enclosure and is sometimes called the offertorial fire because this is where the main offerings are made.

[20] Here the words are *asmad-vidyā* and *ātma-vidyā*, knowledge of us and knowledge of *ātmā*. *Ātmā*, of course, has many meanings and most commentators take this occurrence as "knowledge of Self." I have taken it as a reflective.

descendants will never be destroyed. In both in this world and the next, we protect that person who understands and respects this."

Here ends the Twelfth *Khaṇḍa*

Thirteenth *Khaṇḍa*

The Eastern Fire Instructs

1. The eastern fire[19] next instructed Upakosala; "Breath, space, sky and lightning, these are my forms, and the person you see in lightning, it is I and I alone.

2. "One who understands this becomes freed of bad deeds. Such a person inherits this world and lives a full life with luster. His descendants will never be destroyed. In both in this world and the next, we protect that person who understands and respects this."

Here ends the Thirteenth *Khaṇḍa*

Fourteenth *Khaṇḍa*

The Fires Conclude

1. Together the fires continued, "Upakosala, child, now you have knowledge of us and knowledge of yourself.[20] Your teacher will take it from here." The teacher then arrived and spoke, "Upakosala!"

2. "Yes, sir?" he responded.

"Your face shines as if you have gained knowledge of *brahma*. Who has taught you?" asked the teacher.

As if to conceal the fact, Upakosala responded, "Who could have possibly taught me, sir?" Then looking at the fires, he said, "They look like this now, but previously they looked different."

The teacher asked, "Son, what did they tell you?"

3. "Just this," Upakosala acknowledged.

The teacher responded, "They did indeed teach you the exoteric

---

[21] Here the word is *lokān,* and so the literal translation reads, "They told you about the worlds."

[22] The allusion here is similar to a drop of water on the leaf of the lotus. Water never sticks to the pure lotus leaf, and so the lotus is forever untouched by the stains of this world. Similarly, a drop of ghee or water never clouds the eye, but immediately moves to the edges of the pupil. So it is with the person seen in the eye, the *ātmā.* He is never stained by this world.

[23] The word is *saṃyad-vāma*, "joined with beauty."

[24] The word is *vāma-nī*, "leading beauty."

[25] The word is *bhāma-nī*, "leading light." These are all descriptive names of *brahma*.

[26] During the time of the Rig Veda burial of the dead was the practice, but by the time of the Upanishads cremation had become the standard practice. Here the reason is clear. Fire acted as a vehicle to carry the departed soul on its journey.

side[21] of this knowledge, but I will teach you that part by which you will shed all evil, just as water cannot adhere to the lotus leaf."

"Yes, please teach me, sir."

And so the teacher spoke.

Here ends the Fourteenth *Khaṇḍa*

Fifteenth *Khaṇḍa*

The Path to *Brahma*

1. This One, the person seen in the eye, is the *ātmā*. It is immortal. It is fearless. It is *brahma*. This is why, if one drops melted butter or water into the eye, it immediately goes to the edges.[22]

2. They say it is beauty personified,[23] for all beauty is drawn to this One. And for the man who understands this, all beauty is drawn to him.

3. It is the bestower of beauty,[24] for it bestows all beauty. And for the man who knows this, he too becomes a bestower of all beauty.

4. It is the bringer of light,[25] for it shines in all the worlds. And for the man who knows this, he too shines in all the worlds.

5. Persons who have realized this knowledge, whether their cremation rites are performed or not,[26] enter the flame and go to

the day. From the day they enter the bright side of the lunar month,[27] and from the lunar month they go to the six months when the sun moves north.[28] From there they enter the year, and from the year they enter the sun. From the sun they go to the moon, and finally enter lightning, where they meet a person who is not human, who leads them to *brahma*. The is the path of the gods, the path of *brahma*.[29] Those who follow this path never return to this human condition. Yea, they never return!

Here ends the Fifteenth *Khaṇḍa*

Sixteenth *Khaṇḍa*

The Two Paths Created during Sacrifice

1. The wind purifies. It is sacrifice. As it moves it purifies all

---

[27] The lunar month is divided into two halves, the waxing bright side and the waning dark side. Those leaving this world follow the path of light, and so they enter the two weeks when the moon is waxing.

[28] Like the moon, the sun also has a light side and a dark side. From December to June as the days are becoming longer in the northern hemisphere, the sun is thought to be on its bright side. From June till December the sun is on its dark side as the days are becoming shorter. Persons leaving the world enter the bright side of the sun.

[29] There are two paths, the path of the gods, *deva-yāna*, and the path of the forefathers, *pitṛ-yāna*. The path of the gods described here leads to *brahma*. It is the path of light. The path of the forefathers brings one back to the world. These two paths have been mentioned previously (BU 6.2.15-16). Similarly, in the later tradition these paths are also mentioned (BG 8.24-26).

things; and because it purifies as it moves, it is the sacrifice. It has two paths: mind and speech.

2. One path is created by the *brahmā* priest; the other is created by the other priests, the *hotṛ*, the *adhvaryu* and u*dgātṛ*. During a sacrifice, if the *brahmā* priest interrupts the morning litany before the final mantra is recited, only one path is created; the other is disrupted. If this happens it is like a man trying to walk with only one leg or a cart trying to move with only one wheel. The sacrifice is damaged. And if the sacrifice is damaged, the patron is also damaged. And having sacrificed in this way, the patron actually becomes worse off.

3-4. But if, during a sacrifice, the *brahmā* priest does not interrupt the morning litany before the final mantra is recited, both paths are created and one is not disrupted. When this happens, it is like a man walking on both legs or a cart moving with both wheels. The sacrifice is on firm support. And if the sacrifice is on firm support, the patron is on firm support. And having so sacrificed, the patron benefits.

Here Ends the Sixteenth *Khaṇḍa*

Seventeenth *Khaṇḍa*

Correcting Mistakes during a Sacrifice

1-3. Prajapati, the creator, "cooked down" these worlds, and, as he cooked, he extracted their essences in the form of three gods. From earth he got fire; from sky he got wind; from the heavens he got the sun. He then cooked these gods down and extracted their essences. From fire he got the Rig; from wind he got the Yajur; and from the sun he got the Sama. Finally, he cooked these down and extracted their essences. From the Rig he got *bhūr*; from the Yajur he got *bhuvas;* and from the Sama he got *svar*.[30]

4. During a sacrifice, if a mistake is made with the Rig, one can repair the error by making an oblation into the householder's fire while chanting *bhūr svāḥa*. In this way, using the power of the Rig, one can correct errors relating to the Rig.

5. During a sacrifice, if a mistake is made with the Yajur, one can repair the error by making an oblation into the southern fire while chanting *bhuvaḥ svāḥa*. In this way, using the power of the Yajur, one can correct errors relating to the Yajur.

6. During a sacrifice, if a mistake is made with the Sama, one can repair the error by making an oblation into the eastern fire

---

[30] *Bhūr*, *bhuvas* and *svar* are the three "great utterances," the *vyāhṛtis.* Today, in modern Hinduism, they are still recited at the beginning of the *gāyatrī* and at fire rituals.

[31] The word is *lavaṇa*, which is salt, but it must refer to some other agent that was used to repair gold.

[32] In a *yajña* there are four main priests, the *brahmā*, *hotā*, *adhvaryu* and the *udgātā.* The *brahmā* was the most learned. He may be compared to the conductor of the orchestra.

[33] Literally, "inclines towards the north."

[34] This verse is obscure and open to other interpretations.

while chanting *svaḥ svāḥa*. In this way, using the power of the Sama, one can correct errors relating to the Sama.

7-8. Just as gold can be repaired using salt,[31] silver with gold, tin with silver, lead with tin, iron with lead, and wood with iron or leather, so a sacrifice can be repaired using the power of these worlds, these gods, and these three Vedas. In this way a sacrifice can be corrected. The one who understands this is the *brahmā* priest.[32]

9. That sacrifice becomes most auspicious[33] when there is a *brahmā* priest who knows this. In this regard, there is a hymn about the *brahmā* priest who has this knowledge:

Wherever a fault occurs,
There the *brahmā* goes.
Like a mare, the *brahmā* protects
All those who sacrifice.[34]

10. The *brahmā* priest who knows this protects the sacrifice, his patron, and all the other priests. Therefore, one should choose a *brahmā* priest who knows this and never one who does not.

Here Ends the Seventeenth *Khaṇḍa*

Here Ends the Fourth *Adhyāya*

Fifth *Adhyāya*

First *Khaṇḍa*

Breath: the Oldest and the Greatest[1]

1-5. That person who knows the oldest and greatest becomes the oldest and greatest. Breath is the oldest and greatest. That person who knows what is most excellent becomes the most excellent within his community. Speech is the most excellent. That person who knows the foundation stands firm in both this world and the next. Sight is the foundation. That person who knows wealth has his desires fulfilled, both earthly and divine. Hearing is wealth. That person who knows the resting place becomes the resting place for his community. The mind is the resting place.

6-7. Once upon a time the vital senses argued over who was the best. They called out, "I am the best! I am the best!" Eventually they approached their father, Prajapati, and said, "Reverend sir! Who amongst us is the best?" Prajapati replied, "One by one let each of you step outside of the body. That one among you is best whose body is worse off when you have left it."

8. Speech first stepped outside of the body, wandered abroad for a year and then returned. Upon returning he asked, "So how did you live without me?"

[1] See BU 6.1 and KauU 3.3 for similar stories.

"We lived as the dumb, without speaking, but with breath we breathed, with the eye we saw, with the ear we heard, and with the mind we thought." Speech reentered the body.

9. Next sight stepped outside of the body, wandered abroad for a year and then returned. Upon returning he asked, "So how did you live without me?"

"We lived as the blind, without seeing, but with breath we breathed, with speech we spoke, with the ear we heard, and with the mind we thought." Sight reentered the body.

10. Then hearing stepped outside of the body, wandered abroad for a year and then returned. Upon returning he asked, "So how did you live without me?"

"We lived as the deaf, without hearing, but with breath we breathed, with speech we spoke, with the eye we saw, and with the mind we thought." Hearing reentered the body.

11. The mind then stepped outside of the body, wandered abroad for a year and then returned. Upon returning he asked, "So how did you live without me?"

"We lived as a fool, without thinking, but with breath we breathed, with speech we spoke, with the eye we saw, and with

---

[2] The word here is *prāṇa.* Throughout the Upanishads *prāṇa* is used to mean both the senses as well as breath. Breath is the basis of all the senses.

the ear we heard." Mind reentered the body.

12. Thereupon breath got up to leave and, as he did, shook all the other vital senses from their foundation just as a great stallion tears away from its tether. Immediately all the other vital senses surrounded breath and cried, "Lord, please stay! You are the greatest among us. Do not leave!"

13-14. Speech spoke to breath, "The excellence I possess is your excellence."

Sight spoke, "The foundation I possess is your foundation."

Hearing spoke, "The wealth I possess is your wealth."

Finally mind spoke, "The resting place I possess is your resting place."

15. This is why people say these senses are not speaking, seeing, hearing, or thinking; they are breath. For breath alone is all these things.[2]

Here ends the First *Khaṇḍa*

Second *Khaṇḍa*

The Power of Breath

1. Breath inquired, "What will be my food?"

The senses replied, "Everything from dogs to birds." All this indeed is food for breath. *Ana* is the most basic name for *prāna,*[3] and for one who understands this there is nothing in this world that is not food.

2. Breath further inquired, "What will be my dress?"

The senses replied, "Water will be your dress." Therefore, before and after people eat, they surround their food with water.[4] In this way it is the custom to "dress" food before eating so it should not be naked.

3. Having told this to Goshruti Vaiyaghrapadya, Satyakama Jabala said, "This knowledge is so powerful that if it was told to a dried old stump it would surely grow branches with fresh green leaves!"

4. If one desires greatness, he should consecrate himself on the night of the new moon. On the subsequent full moon night, he should prepare a mixture of herbs, yogurt and honey, which he offers into the fire with clarified butter while chanting,

---

[3] The word *prāṇa* is made of *pra* + *ana*. *Pra* is a prefix which, when added to a noun, suggests greatness or increase. Thus *pra* + *ana* suggests a meaning of "great breath."

[4] This is the source of the *brāhmaṇa* practice of encircling a meal with water and sipping water before and after a meal.

[5] Literally, *amo namāsi, amā hi te sarvam idam,* "You are *ama* by name, for all this is your *amā.*" Here there are two words, *ama* and *amā. Ama* is taken as "power" or "life force" and *amā* is taken as "without measure."

[6] RV 5.82.1.

"*Jyeṣṭhāya svāhā, śreṣṭhāya svāha,* glory to the Oldest, glory to the Best." Then, with each oblation he should keep a few drops and make a potion.

5. Continuing he should chant "*Vasiṣṭhāya svāhā* (Glory to the Most Excellent)!" and keep a few drops for the potion; then "*Pratisthāya svāhā,* (Glory to the Foundation)!" and keep a few drops for the potion; then "*Saṃpade svāhā,* (Glory to Wealth)!" and keep a few drops for the potion; and finally, "*Āyatanāya svāhā,* (Glory to the Resting Place)!" and keep a few drops for the potion.

6. Stepping back from the fire and holding the potion up in cupped hands, let him repeat aloud "You are life force without measure. You are all things.[5] And as you are the oldest, the best, and the sovereign lord, may I become the oldest, the best, and the sovereign lord. May I be all this."

7. Let him then recite the following Rig verse[6] and sip the potion at the end of each quarter:

tat-savitur vṛṇīmahe (sip the potion);
vayaṃ devasya bhojanam (sip the potion);
śreṣṭhaṃ sarva-dhātamam (sip the potion);
turaṃ bhagasya dhīmahi (sip the remainder of the potion).

8. Having washed the goblet or vessel, let him lay on a skin, or just bare ground, to the west of the fire and remain silent and composed. If he should see a woman in his dreams, he will

know the procedure has been successful.

9. In this regard there is the following verse:

"During the performance of a sacred rite,
If a man sees a woman in his dreams,
He should know it is a sign of success.
Indeed, it is a sign of success."

Here ends the Second *Khaṇḍa*

Third *Khaṇḍa*

Instruction to Gautama Begins

Once upon a time, Shvetaketu, the son of Aruni, arrived at the assembly of Pancala. There Pravahana Jaivali, the king of the Pancala, spoke to him: "Son, have you been instructed?"[7]

"Yes, sir!" Shvetaketu replied.

2. "Do you know where beings go when they leave this world?"

"No, sir."

"Do you know how they return?"

"No, sir."

---

[7] See BU 6.2 for a similar discussion.

"Do you know the differences between the path of the gods and the path of the ancestors?"

"No, sir."

3. "Do you know why the world up there does not fill up?"

"No, sir."

"Do you know how water speaks with a human voice after the fifth oblation?"

"No, sir. Not even this."

4-5. "You said you had been instructed, but you do not know these things? How can you call yourself educated?"

In distress, Shvetaketu ran home to his father, Gautama, and said, "Venerable father, you said I had been educated, but in fact I have not. That excuse for a king asked me five questions, but I could not answer even a single one"

Gautama replied, "As you have stated these questions to me, I too do not know the answers. Had I known, I would have instructed you!"

6. Thereupon Gautama went to the king. Arriving, he was shown proper respect. Then, in the morning, he appeared in the same assembly as his son. The king spoke to him: "Respected sir, choose a boon of earthly riches!"

Gautama replied, "O King, keep your earthly wealth. Instead, kindly answer the questions you asked my son." The king became filled with anxiety.

7. "Stay with me for some time and I will teach you," he commanded. He then said, "Gautama, as you have rightly said, this knowledge has never been known to *brāhmanas*. It has been in the possession of the ruling class alone. But now listen as I tell you."

Here ends the Third *Khaṇḍa*

Fourth *Khaṇḍa*

The Heavens are Fire

1-2. "The world up there is a fire, O Gautama. The sun is the fuel. Its rays are smoke. The day is the flame. The moon is its burning coals. The constellations are the sparks. And into that fire the gods offer faith, and from that fire King Soma comes forth."

Here Ends the Fourth *Khaṇḍa*

Fifth *Khaṇḍa*

Rain is a Fire

1-2. "Rain is a fire, O Gautama. The wind is its fuel. The cloud is the smoke. Lightning is the flame. The thunderbolt is its burning coals. Hail is the sparks. And into that fire the gods offer King Soma, and from that offering rains come forth."

Sixth *Khaṇḍa*
The Earth is a Fire

1-2. "The earth is a fire, O Gautama. The year is its fuel. Space is the smoke. The night is the flame. The directions are its burning coals. The intermediate regions are the sparks. And into that fire the gods offer rains, and from that offering food comes forth."

Seventh *Khaṇḍa*
A Man is a Fire

1-2. "A man is a fire, O Gautama. Speech is his fuel. Breath is the smoke. His tongue is the flame. His eyes are the burning coals. His ears are the sparks. And into that fire the gods offer food, and from that offering semen comes forth."

Here Ends the Seventh *Khaṇḍa*

Eighth *Khaṇḍa*
A Woman is a Fire

1-2. "A woman is a fire, O Gautama. Her waist is the fuel. When she comes close, that is her smoke. Her vagina is the flame. Penetration is the burning coals. Her sexual joy is the sparks. And into that fire the gods offer semen, and from that offering an embryo comes forth."

Here Ends the Eighth *Khaṇḍa*

Ninth *Khaṇḍa*

The Course of Man

1-2. "So this is how water becomes the voice of a man after the fifth oblation. After being in the womb for nine or tenth months, a man is born. He then lives his allotted lifespan, after which he is taken to fire, the very fire from which he has born."

Here Ends the Eighth *Khaṇḍa*

Tenth *Khaṇḍa*

Ways of Leaving the World

1-2. When they depart this life, the wilderness dwellers who have renounced this world, whose faith is founded on austerity,

---

[8] To leave this world during the times of light is most important. Therefore, everything described here is in terms of increased illumination. The lunar month has two halves, a waxing half and a waning half. The waxing fortnight is more important than the waning fortnight. Similarly, the six months of the year from December to June, when days are getting longer, is more important than the following six months from July to December, when the days are getting shorter.

[9] Here the idea of *punya* is referenced. One lives in this world and performs good deeds to accumulate merit, *punya*. This *punya* eventually bears fruit so that, in a future life, good fortune will result. The moon is seen as a heavenly world in which one can enjoy residing only so long as one has sufficient merit to remain there. But once that merit is used up, one must leave and return to this earthly realm.

enter the flame at the time of cremation and proceed to the day. From the day they enter the light of the waxing moon, after which they go to the six months of the year when the sun is moving north.[8] After this they proceed to the year and then to the sun. From the sun they enter the moon, and from there they enter lightning. In lightning they meet a being who is not human, who takes them on to *brahma*. This is *devāyana*, the path of gods.

3-6. On the other hand, those who dwell in the village, who follow the worldly path of sacrifice and charity, enter smoke at the time of cremation and go to the night. From the night they proceed to the waning light of the moon, and from there enter the six months of the year when the sun is moving south. After this, however, they do not attain the year. Instead, they attain the world of the ancestors and from there enter space. From space they proceed to the moon, which is King Soma, the food of the gods. This they enjoy only so long as they have merit.[9] When that is exhausted, they return to this world—first to space, then to wind, then to smoke and then to mist—and, finally, to the rain cloud wherein they rain down into this world. In this world they spring up as rice, barley, plants, trees, sesame and beans. This is a difficult situation from which to emerge, for only when someone eats them as food and emits them as semen can they become a being again.

7. Those whose behavior has been pious can expect to enter favorable wombs as they reenter this world. A birth in the family of a brahmin, a kshatriya or a vaishya is favorable. Those whose

behavior has been impious enter base wombs, like those of dogs, pigs and outcastes.[10]

8. But there are others, worse still, who follow neither of these paths, who become tiny and insignificant creatures who repeatedly take birth and die in this world. This is the third situation. And for this reason the world up there never fills up. One should guard against falling into this situation. In this regard there is the following verse:

A gold thief, a drunkard, a man who sleeps with his teacher's wife, and the murderer of a brahmin,
These four sink down in this world,
As does the man who consorts with these evildoers.

Yet, the one who understands the significance of these five fires is not stained with evil even though he may consort with these evildoers. Indeed, the man who has this knowledge becomes pure, good, and attains the worlds of the pious.

Here ends the Tenth *Khaṇḍa*

---

[10] Here the idea of *pāpa* is suggested. This is the counterpart to *punya*. If one lives an evil life, he accumulates *pāpa*, negative merit, which pulls one into hellish situations of life to suffer until this *pāpa* is used up.

[11] For a parallel version of this story, see SB 10.6.1.

[12] Here the expression is *vaiśvanara ātmā*. The word *vaiśvānara* means "common to all" or "universal." So here and in the following chapters, 5.12 to 5.18, the discussion will be about the *ātmā* that is common to all, a universal soul.

Eleventh *Khaṇḍa*[11]

Dialogue on the Universal *Ātmā* Begins

1. Pracinashala, the son of Upamanyu; Satyayajna, the son of Pulusha; Indradyumna, the grandson of Bhallavi; Jana, the son of Sharkarakshya; and Budila, the son of Ashvatarashva, were all learned and wealthy householders who came together to discuss the questions of the day: "What is our *ātmā? What is brahma?"*

2. They reached the following conclusion: "Sirs, there is one gentleman, Uddalaka, son of Aruna, who is studying the universal *ātmā.*[12] Let us go to him." They went to him.

3-4. Seeing them coming, Uddalaka thought to himself "These wealthy and learned gentlemen will question me, but I do not have the answers to all their questions, so let me refer them to another." So he said to them, "Sirs, there is one gentleman, Ashvapati Kaikeya, who is currently studying this universal *ātmā*. Let us all go to him!" They went to him.

5. Ashvapati greeted them appropriately and then, in the morning, said to them, "In my kingdom there are no thieves, misers, drunkards, or anyone without education or a sacrificial fire. We do not even have lechers not to mention loose women! Good Sirs, I am about to sacrifice. Join me. I will award you the same gifts as the priests. Be with me!"

6. They replied to him, "When a person comes with a specific purpose, it is best to speak sooner than later. You have been studying the universal *ātmā*. Please speak to us about this."

7. Ashvapati responded, "Come in the morning; I will speak." So in the morning they went to him, fuel in hand,[13] and even without initiating them, he began to speak.

Here ends the Eleventh *Khaṇḍa*

Twelfth *Khaṇḍa*

The Sky as the Universal *Ātmā*

1-2 Ashvapati asked the son of Upamanyu, "What is it that you venerate as *ātmā*?"

"The sky, my Lord;" he replied.

"Since you venerate this brightly shining one (*sutejas)* as the universal *ātmā,* there is always the pressing of *soma* in your family.[14] You eat food. You see beauty. Indeed, for one who venerates the universal *ātmā* in this way, there is always food, beauty, and knowledge in their family. But this is only the head of the *ātmā*. Had you not come to me, your head would have shattered!"

---

[13] "Fuel in hand" means they adopted a humble attitude and approached as students.

[14] Here three pressings of *soma* are mentioned, *suta*, *prasuta*, and *āsuta*. This corresponds to the morning, afternoon and evening extractions of the *soma* plant.

Here ends the Twelfth *Khaṇḍa*

Thirteenth *Khaṇḍa*

The Sun as the Universal *Ātmā*

1-2 Ashvapati then asked Satyayajna, the son of Pulusha, "What is it that you venerate as the *ātmā*?"

"The sun, my Lord;" he replied.

"Since you venerate this many splendored one *(viśva-rūpa)* as the universal *ātmā,* there is always great splendor in your family. You have gold ornaments, vehicles, female servants and wealth. You eat food. You see beauty. Indeed, for one who venerates the universal *ātmā* in this way, there is always food, beauty, and knowledge in their family. But this is only the eye of the *ātmā*. Had you not come to me, you would have become blind!"

Here ends the Thirteenth *Khaṇḍa*

Fourteenth *Khaṇḍa*

The Wind as the Universal *Ātmā*

1-2 Ashvapati then asked Indradyumna, the grandson of Bhallavi, "What is it that you venerate as the *ātmā*?"

"The wind, my Lord;" he replied.

"Since you venerate this one with many paths, the wind, as the universal *ātmā,* there are always gifts[15] coming from many sources in your family. You have rows and rows of chariots. You eat food. You see beauty. Indeed, for one who venerates the universal *ātmā* in this way, there is always food, beauty and knowledge in their family. But this is only the breath of the *ātmā*. Had you not come to me your breath would have left you!"

Here ends the Fourteenth *Khaṇḍa*

Fifteenth *Khaṇḍa*

Space as the Universal *Ātmā*

1-2 Ashvapati then asked Jana, the son of Sharkarakshya, "What is it that you venerate as the *ātmā*?"

"Space, my Lord;" he replied.

"Since you venerate the abundant one, space, as the universal *ātmā,* you are always replete with offspring and property. You eat food. You see beauty. Indeed, for one who venerates the universal *ātmā* in this way, there is always food, beauty, and knowledge in their family. But this is only the body of the *ātmā*. Had you not come to me, your body would have disintegrated!"

---

[15] The word is *bali*, which is a gift or tribute given as a sacrificial offering to a priest.

[16] The word is *rayi*, which could also be taken as property.

[17] Here the word is *baṣṭi*, which could also be taken as bladder or lower abdomen.

Here ends the Fifteenth *Khaṇḍa*

Sixteenth *Khaṇḍa*

Water as the Universal *Ātmā*

1-2 Ashvapati then asked Budila, the son of Ashvatarashva, "What is it that you venerate as the *ātmā*?"

"Water, my Lord;" he replied.

Since you venerate waters[16] as the universal *ātmā*, you are always replete with wealth and increase. You eat food. You see beauty. Indeed, for one who venerates the universal *ātmā* in this way, there is always food, beauty and knowledge in their family. But this is only the stomach[17] of the *ātmā*. Had you not come to me, your stomach would have exploded!"

Here ends the Sixteenth *Khaṇḍa*

Seventeenth *Khaṇḍa*

The Earth as the Universal *Ātmā*

1-2 Ashvapati finally asked Uddalaka Aruni, "O Gautama, what is it that you venerate as the *ātmā*?"

"The earth, my Lord;" he replied.

"Since you venerate a firm foundation, the earth, as the universal *ātmā,* you always have a firm foundation of offspring and livestock. You eat food. You see beauty. Indeed, for one who venerates the universal *ātmā* in this way, there is always food, beauty and knowledge in their family. But this is only the feet of the *ātmā*. Had you not come to me, your feet would have withered away!"

Here ends the Seventeenth *Khaṇḍa*

Eighteenth *Khaṇḍa*

The *Ātmā* is beyond Measure

1. Ashvapati then addressed them all: "You are all learned men

[18] The words here are *prādeśa-matram abhivimānam ātmānam*, that the *ātmā* is both a certain measure and without measure. *Prādeśa-matram* is a span, which sometimes is described as the measure from the tip of the thumb to the tip of the forefinger, or about eight inches. In later Hinduism there is reference to the meditation of *paramātmā* over the region of the heart, covering a span of about eight inches. Here a span could be any other distance. Some commentators suggest the distance from the earth to the sky.

[19] In this section, CU 5-19 through CU 5-23, feeding the five vital breaths is mentioned through offerings into the fire. All this is premised on the understanding that the universe "out there" relates to the universe inside the individual. Feed the universe out there and you are feeding the universe within. In other words, there is a universe out there which corresponds to the universe inside the individual, and when these breaths of the universe are fed, they are also fed within for the performers of the fire sacrifice. Thus the fire is the means of linking these two universes. And similarly, when an enlightened man feeds himself, he also feeds the vital airs of the universe. That is to say, when a *brahmaṇa* eats the whole world eats.

who see the universal *ātmā* in distinct ways, as you have described, and therefore you eat food. But for one who venerates this universal *ātmā* as both measuring a span as well as beyond all measure,[18] that person eats food in all worlds, in all beings, and in all souls."

2. Here is how we describe this universal *ātmā*: Its head is this brightly shining one, its eye is the many splendored one, its breath is the one with many paths, its body is the abundant one, its stomach is wealth, its feet is the earth, its chest is the sacrificial altar, its hair is the sacred *kuśa* grass, its heart is the householder's fire, its mind is the southern fire, and its mouth is the eastern fire.

Here Ends the Eighteenth *Khaṇḍa*

Nineteenth *Khaṇḍa*

The First Offering

1-2. With this understanding, the first portion of food[19] should be offered into the fire with the chant "*Prāṇāya svaha*." Thus, the *prāṇa* breath is satisfied. And when the *prāṇa* breath is satisfied, sight is satisfied; and when sight is satisfied, the sun is satisfied; and when the sun is satisfied, the sky is satisfied; and when the sky is satisfied, whatever is under the sky and the sun is satisfied. And when all these are satisfied, the man with children, livestock, food, fame and sacred learning is also satisfied.

Here Ends the Nineteenth *Khaṇḍa*

Twentieth *Khaṇḍa*

The Second Offering

1-2. With this understanding, the second portion of food should be offered into the fire with the chant "*Vyānāya svaha.*" Thus the *vyāna* breath is satisfied. And when the *vyāna* breath is satisfied, hearing is satisfied; and when hearing is satisfied, the moon is satisfied; and when the moon is satisfied, the directions are satisfied; and when the directions are satisfied, whatever is under the directions and the moon is satisfied. And when all these are satisfied, the man with children, livestock, food, fame and sacred learning is also satisfied.

Here Ends the Twentieth *Khaṇḍa*

Twenty-first *Khaṇḍa*

The Third Offering

1-2. With this understanding, the third portion of food should be offered into the fire with the chant "*Apānāya svaha.*" Thus, the *apāna* breath is satisfied. And when the *apāna* breath is satisfied, speech is satisfied; and when speech is satisfied, fire is satisfied; and when fire is satisfied, the earth is satisfied; and when the earth is satisfied, whatever the earth and fire oversee is satisfied. And when all these are satisfied, the man with children, livestock, food, fame and sacred learning is also satisfied.

Here Ends the Twenty-first *Khaṇḍa*

Twenty-second *Khaṇḍa*

The Fourth Offering

1-2. With this understanding, the fourth portion of food should be offered into the fire with the chant "*Samānāya svaha.*" Thus, the *samāna* breath is satisfied. And when the *samāna* breath is satisfied, the mind is satisfied; and when the mind is satisfied, rains are satisfied; and when rains are satisfied, lightning is satisfied; and when lightning is satisfied, whatever lightning and rains oversee is satisfied. And when all these are satisfied, the man with children, livestock, food, fame and sacred learning is also satisfied.

Here Ends the Twenty-second *Khaṇḍa*

Twenty-third *Khaṇḍa*

The Fifth Offering

1-2. With this understanding, the fifth portion of food should be offered into the fire with the chant "*Udānāya svaha.*" Thus, the *udāna* breath is satisfied. And when the *udāna* breath is satisfied, the wind is satisfied; and when the wind is satisfied, space is satisfied; and when space is satisfied, whatever wind and space oversee is satisfied. And when all these are satisfied the man with children, livestock, food, fame and sacred learning is also satisfied.

Here Ends the Twenty-third *Khaṇḍa*

Twenty-fourth *Khaṇḍa*

The Importance of Knowledge

1-2. If a person performs a fire sacrifice without this understanding, it is like making the offering into the ashes, without the coals. On the other hand, when a fire sacrifice is performed by a learned man with the proper understanding, his offering is made to all the worlds, all beings, and all souls.

3-4. When the fire sacrifice is performed by a man of learning, all his sins are burned up just as the tips of sacred grass are burned up during a fire sacrifice.[20] Even if a learned man should offer the remnants of his food to an outcaste that would still be an offering to the universal soul.[21] In this regard there is the following verse:

5. As hungry children sit close to their mother,
So all beings sit near the fire sacrifice.
Indeed, they sit near the fire sacrifice!

Here ends the Twenty-fourth *Khaṇḍa*

Here Ends the Fifth *Adhyāya*

---

[20] There is a special kind of grass called *kuśa*, which is used in the fire sacrifice. The tips of this grass are commonly ignited and allowed to burn so the ash falls into the clarified butter.

[21] See fn to CU 5.19.1 The rules of caste and purity forbid a low-caste person from eating with a high-caste person, but for an enlightened person these rules do not apply. In fact, a *brāhmaṇa* is so powerful that, when he eats, the whole world eats, and even if an outcaste eats the remnants of a *brāhmaṇa,* the whole universe eats.

Sixth *Adhyāya*

First *Khaṇḍa*

Teachings to Shvetaketu Begins

1. There was a boy, Shvetaketu by name, grandson of Aruna. Once upon a time, his father spoke to him: "Shvetaketu, my child, it is time to live the life of a sacred student, a *brahmacharī.* There has never been anyone in our family who has not studied and who is a *brāhmaṇa* in name only."[1]

2-3. So Shvetaketu left home at age 12 and returned at 24, and, having studied all the Vedas, he had become haughty, arrogant, and proud of his learning. Again his father spoke to him:"Shvetaketu, my child, now that you have studied and have become haughty, arrogant and proud of your learning, did you learn that teaching by which what is unheard becomes heard, what is unthought becomes thought, and what is unknown becomes known?"

"No, sir. Pray tell me that teaching."

---

[1] The expression, *brahma-bandhu*, is literally "friend of a *brāhmaṇa*." There is a similar expression *rājanya-bandhu*, "friend of a prince," used in BU 6.2.3. The wider implication is that being a *brāhmaṇa* was not by virtue of birth, but a function of learning. This suggests that, at the time of the Upanishads, one's caste was based on qualities and not birth.

4. His father began: "Know that all things made of clay can be known by a single ball of clay–their difference being in name only, arising from speech[2]–because in truth both are clay.

5. "Know that all things made of copper can be known by a single ornament of copper–their difference being in name only,

---

[2] The words here are *vācārambhanam vikāro nāmadheyam*. This expression has been the subject of much interpretation. *Vācārambhanam* is *vācā ārambhanam,* which is literally "held by speech." This is sometimes translated as "verbal handle." I have rendered it as "arising from speech." The word *vikāra* here has been glossed as "difference," but it could also be taken as "change," "modification," or "transformation." *Nāmadheyam* is name.

[3] The words for existence and non-existence are *sat* and *asat*. Here *sat* is translated as existence, but it could also have been translated as the real, or being. *Asat* is the opposite. Regardless, *sat* is always something positive and *asat* something negative. So the debate has been which came first, *sat* or *asat*, the positive or the negative. RV 10.129 says neither. CU 3.19 presents the view that *asat* came before *sat*. RV 10.72.2 also mentions this view. Instead of just meaning "nothing," *asat* may also refer to a time in the primordial universe when all was influx and chaos, a time before distinct forms emerged. *Sat* therefore refers to the world of order and distinct forms, the physical world we see around us. In modern Hinduism *sat* is generally used to refer to spiritual reality, the soul and God–whatever is permanent, pure and unchanging—whereas *asat* refers to matter and the physical world that is constantly changing and is impermanent. In the early Upanishads this physical world is called *sat* because it is real and tangible and something good. Thus, a major shift has occurred in the meaning of these two words.

arising from speech–because in truth both are copper.

6. "Know that all things made of iron can be known by a single nail cutter–their difference being in name only, arising from speech–because in truth both are iron. This, my child, is the teaching."

7. Shvetaketu said, "It seems these honorable gentlemen did not know this teaching, for had they known they would have surely taught me."

His father continued.

Here ends the First *Khaṇḍa*

Second *Khaṇḍa*

The Creation of the World

1. "In the beginning there was existence alone, one without a second. Others, however, say that in the beginning there was only non-existence, one without a second. And therefore, from non-existence, existence arose.[3]

2. "But how can this be? How can existence possibly come from non-existence? No, in the beginning, my child, there was existence alone, one without a second.

3. "Existence then saw that it was alone and so thought, 'Let me become many!' It emitted heat. Then heat saw that it was alone

and so thought, 'Let me become many.' It emitted water. Therefore, whenever a man grieves, he sweats—from heat water is produced. Water then saw that it was alone and so thought, "Let me become many." It emitted food. Therefore, whenever it rains, food in the form of grains is produced. And so it is from water that grains are produced."

Here ends the Second *Khaṇḍa*

Third *Khaṇḍa*

The Three Divinities and Name and Form

1-3. "In this world beings arise from three sources: eggs, other living creatures, and sprouts.[4] That divinity then thought, 'Let me enter these three with my living self and let me create name and form.[5] In fact, let me make each of them threefold.' So, that divinity entered these three with his living self and created name and form.

---

[4] The AU mentions a fourth source, *svedaja*, born from sweat.

[5] The words used here are *nāma-rūpa*, name and form. This indicates individuality.

[6] Three basic elements–fire, water and earth–are mentioned in this chapter. They have also been called divinities. Red comes from the element fire, white from water, and dark shades from earth. In later *sāṅkhya* philosophy these basic elements become the three underlying constituents of matter (the *triguṇas* of *prakṛti): sattva, rājas* and *tamas*.

[7] The word used here is *anna*, which is literally food.

4. "It made each of them threefold. Learn from me, my son, how each of these has become threefold."

Here ends the Third *Khaṇḍa*

Fourth *Khaṇḍa*

The Three Elements: Fire, Water and Earth

1. "The red color in fire comes from the subtle element fire.[6] The white color in fire comes from the element water. The dark color in fire comes from the element earth.[7] Knowing this, "fire-ness" vanishes, and one understands the appearance of fire as name only, arising from speech. In truth, there are just the basic elements: fire, water and earth.

2. "The red color of the sun comes from the subtle element fire. The white color comes from the element water. The dark color comes from the element earth. Knowing this, "sun-ness" vanishes, and one understands the appearance of the sun as name only, arising from speech. In truth, there are just the basic elements: fire, water and earth.

3. "The red color of the moon comes from the subtle element fire. The white color comes from the element water. The dark color comes from the element earth. Knowing this, "moon-ness" vanishes and one understands the appearance of the moon as name only, arising from speech. In truth, there are just the basic elements: fire, water and earth.

4. "The red color of lightning comes from the subtle element fire. The white color comes from the element water. The dark color comes from the element earth. Knowing this, "lightning-ness" vanishes, and one understands the appearance of lightning as name only, arising from speech. In truth, there are just the basic elements: fire, water and earth.

5. "In the past this is what the wealthy and learned householders knew when they declared, 'No one will now be able to bring up to us what has not been heard, thought or understood.' In knowing these three elements, they knew everything.

6-7. "They knew that whatever appeared red was from the element fire, whatever appeared white was from the element water, and whatever appeared dark was from the element earth. And whatever appeared indistinct they knew was derived from a combination of these divinities.

"Now learn from me, my son, how each of these divinities become threefold when they enter a man."

Here Ends the Fourth *Khaṇḍa*

---

[8] Here, as in the previous chapter, the word is *tejas*, which is literally heat. What is meant is oils, butter and fats that generate heat within the body.

Fifth *Khaṇḍa*

The Composition of a Body

1-3. "Food eaten becomes threefold. The part that is coarsest becomes feces, the middle part becomes flesh, and the finest part becomes mind. Liquids drunk become threefold. The part that is coarsest becomes urine, the middle part becomes blood, and the finest part becomes breath. Fire[8] eaten becomes threefold. The coarsest part becomes bone, the middle part becomes marrow, and the finest part becomes speech.

4. "My son, mind is made of food, breath is made of water, and speech is made of fire."

"Please tell me more, good sir."

"Yes, my son," the father replied.

Here ends the Fifth *Khaṇḍa*

Sixth *Khaṇḍa*

The Composition of a Body Continued

1-4 "When milk is churned, the finest part rises up. It is butter. Similarly, my son, when food is eaten, the finest part rises up and becomes mind. When water is drunk, the finest part rises up and becomes breath. When fire is eaten, the finest part rises up and becomes speech.

5. "Mind is made of food, my son, breath is made of water, and speech is made of fire."

"Please tell me more, good sir."

"Yes, my son," his father replied.

Here ends the Sixth *Khaṇḍa*

Seventh *Khaṇḍa*

A Person is Made of Sixteen Parts

1. Shvetaketu's father said, "A person is made of sixteen parts, my son. For fifteen days do not eat, but drink as much as you wish. Breath is derived from water; so as long as you drink your breath will not be cut off."

2. Shvetaketu fasted for fifteen days and then he approached his father. "What shall I say, sir?"

His father commanded, "Recite Rig, Yajur and Sama verses."

Shvetaketu replied, "I can't remember them, sir."

3. His father replied, "After a big fire, a single remaining ember just the size of a firefly can hardly burn anything. Similarly, even though only one of your sixteen parts remains, you cannot recite the Vedas. Go eat, and then return and learn from me."

4. Shvetaketu ate and then returned to his father. He was then able to recite everything his father asked.

5. His father then said, "After a fire, if a single ember just the size of a firefly remains, it will grow into a big fire once again if straw is placed on that ember. In the same way, my son, if just one of your sixteen parts remains and then food is eaten, your fire will blaze again. This is why you can now recite the Vedas: For the mind is made of food, breath is made of water, and speech is made of fire."

This is what Shvetaketu learned from his father.

Here Ends the Seventh *Khaṇḍa*

Eighth *Khaṇḍa*

The Nature of Sleep

1. Uddalaka Aruni spoke to his son, Shvetaketu: "Learn from me, my son, the nature of sleep. When a person has entered into deep sleep, he is united with Being (*sat*). He has gone into himself; and therefore we say he is sleeping when he has gone into himself.

2. "As a tethered bird tries to fly in every direction, but is unable to go anywhere and so eventually comes to rest on its very tether, similarly the mind tries to go in every direction, but, being unable to find shelter, eventually takes shelter on the breath. For breath is the tether of the mind.

3. "Hear from me, my son, the relationship between hunger and thirst. When a person desires to eat—in other words, when he is hungry—he must lead his food with water.[9] In this way, as we speak of the leader of cows, the leader of horses and the leader of men, so water is the leader of food.

---

[9] In order to swallow food, there must at least be a little liquid in the mouth to act as lubrication. This is why it is recommended to sip a little water before eating. For this reason, water is said to be a "leader" of food.

[10] In other words, "this body."

[11] This is the famous *tat tvam asi* statement. The full statement in Sanskrit reads *sa ya eṣo 'ṇim aitad ātmyam idaṃ sarvam/ tat satyam/ sa ātmātattvamasi/.* This famous passage has been used by commentators to show the identity of the individual soul and the universal soul. The usual translation of *tat tvam asi* is "that you are," where the pronoun *tat* "that" has been construed with *tvam*, "you." This is the basis of Shankara's Advaita Vedanta, which describes the unity of all things as *brahma.*

One interesting variation comes from the followers of the dvaita school headed by Madhvacharya where they divide the words *sa ātmātat tvam asi* as *sa ātmā* ***atat*** *tvam asi,* "that you are not." This slight change in how the *sandhi* is dissolved within *ātmātat* changes the meaning completely. This expression becomes one of the pivotal expressions in Hindu theology, creating the three main schools of Vedanta theology: *advaita*, *dvaita*, and *viśiṣṭha-advaita.*

However, there is a major grammatical issue that affects this expression. In the last part of this statement, *tat tvam asi*, *tat* (that) is a neuter pronoun while *tvam* (you) is masculine and therefore *tat* and *tvam* cannot, strictly speaking, be construed with each other and so cannot be translated as "that you are" (continued page 126)

"Understand how this bud[10] has arisen. It could never exist without a root.

4. "Other than food, what else could be the root? Similarly, my son, with food as the bud, look for water as the root; with water as the bud, look for heat as the root; with heat as the bud, look for Being (*sat*) as the root. For Being is the root of all creatures. Being is their resting place; Being is their foundation.

5. Similarly, when a person desires to drink, heat first leads what is drunk. And just as there is a leader of cows, a leader of horses and a leader of men, heat is the leader of water.

"Understand how this bud has arisen. It could never exist without a root.

6. "Other than water, my son, what else could be the root? Similarly, with water as the bud, look for heat as the root; with heat as the bud, look for Being (*sat*) as the root. Being is the root of all creatures. Being is their resting place; Being is their foundation. I have already described to you how each of these three divinities becomes threefold as they enter a man. Indeed, when a man is dying his speech returns to mind, his mind returns to breath, his breath returns to heat, and his heat returns to the highest divinity.

7. "That which is the finest essence of things, that is the soul of all. It is the essence of Being. It is the *ātmā,* and you are like that, O Shvetaketu![11]

"Please tell me more, sir."

"My child, let me continue."

Here ends the Eighth *Khaṇḍa*

Ninth *Khaṇḍa*

Teachings to Shvetaketu Continued

1-3. "As bees, my son, collect the pollens of various trees and make it into one mixture, the individual particles of pollen do not discriminate: 'I am the essence of this tree,' 'I am the essence of that tree.' Similarly, when all these creatures enter Being, they do not think 'We have entered Being.' Whatever they were in this world—a tiger, a lion, a wolf, a boar, a fly, a moth, a gnat or a mosquito—they all enter Being.

4. "That which is the finest essence of things, that is the soul of all. It is the essence of Being. It is the *ātmā,* and you are like that, O Shvetaketu!"

---

or "that you are not." To be properly written the expression should be read, ***sa*** *tvam asi*, where *sa* is masculine agreeing with *tvam* which is also masculine. All traditional commentators ignore this fact. The solution to this problem is to take the word *tat* as an adverb instead of a pronoun. This gives *tat* the sense of "therefore" or "because of this." This how I have translated the expression.

"Please tell me more, sir."

"My child, let me continue."

Here ends the Ninth *Khaṇḍa*

Tenth *Khaṇḍa*

Teachings to Shvetaketu Continued

1-2. "These rivers–the eastern ones and the western ones–they actually both come from the ocean and then they return to the ocean. Indeed, they are the ocean. Yet, while they are in the ocean they do not know 'I am the waters of this river,' 'I am the waters of that river.' In the same way, my son, when all these creatures enter Being, they do not think 'We have entered Being.' Whatever they were in this world—a tiger, a lion, a wolf, a boar, a fly, a moth, a gnat or a mosquito—they all enter Being.

3. "That which is the finest essence of things, that is the soul of all. It is the essence of Being. It is the *ātmā,* and you are like that, O Shvetaketu!"

"Please tell me more, sir."

"My child, let me continue."

Here ends the Tenth *Khaṇḍa*

Eleventh *Khaṇḍa*

Teachings to Shvetaketu Continued

1-2 "My child, if someone should strike at the root of this great tree, life-sap will flow. If someone should strike in the middle of this tree, life-sap will flow; and if someone should strike at the top of this tree, life-sap will flow. Pervaded by the essence of life, this great tree stands tall, drinking and rejoicing. But if this life essence should leave a single branch, the branch would immediately wither; and if this life essence should leave a second branch, it too would wither; and the same for a third branch. Indeed, when it leaves the entire tree, the whole tree withers.

3. "In this same way, my son, when this life energy departs, the body[12] dies, but life itself does not die.

"That which is the finest essence of things, that is the soul of all. It is the essence of Being. It is the *ātmā,* and you are like that, O Shvetaketu!"

"Please tell me more, sir."

"My child, let me continue."

Here Ends the Eleventh *Khaṇḍa*

---

[12] The word is *idam,* "this." Here it has been glossed as "the body," but it could also refer to any living entity.

Twelfth *Khaṇḍa*

Teachings to Shvetaketu Continued

1-3 “Bring the fruit of that banyan tree.”

“Here it is, sir.”

“Split it open.”

“It is split, sir.”

“What do you see?”

“These tiny seeds, sir.”

“Split one of them open.”

“It is split, sir.”

“What do you see?”

“I do not see anything, sir.”

Uddalaka then told him, “Even though you do not see anything, a great banyan tree has grown from this finest essence! Believe me, my son, that which is the finest essence of things, that is the soul of all. It is the essence of Being. It is the *ātmā,* and you are like that, O Shvetaketu!”

"Please tell me more, sir."

"My child, let me continue."

Here Ends the Twelfth *Khaṇḍa*

Thirteenth *Khaṇḍa*
Teachings to Shvetaketu Continued

"Put this salt into water and return to me in the morning." Shvetaketu did so. Then his father told him, "Bring me the salt you placed into the water." Groping the water, the boy found nothing. It had dissolved.

His father said, "Now take a sip of the water from this end. How does it taste?"

"Salty."

"Now sip from that end. How does it taste?"

"Salty."

"Now throw the water aside and return later." Shvetaketu did

---

[13] The word *ācārya* is used here for teacher. Throughout the Upanishads a teacher is considered essential as the remover of the "blindfold." The teacher is even considered superior to parents.

so and found that the salt was still there. His father then said, "You could not perceive it, my son, but it was always there.

"That which is the finest essence of things, that is the soul of all. It is the essence of Being. It is the *ātmā,* and you are like that, O Shvetaketu!"

"Please tell me more, sir."

"My child, let me continue."

Here Ends the Thirteenth *Khaṇḍa*

Fourteenth *Khaṇḍa*

Teachings to Shvetaketu Continued

1-2. "My son, consider a man who has been brought blindfolded to a deserted place. He will call out to the east, the north, and the south. But if someone should remove his blindfold and tell him, 'Go this way to Gandhara, he will go from village to village asking the way; and being wise and intelligent, he will eventually find his way home. In the same way, a man in this world, who has a teacher[13] knows I am delayed only until I am freed of my ignorance, then I will arrive.

3. 'That which is the finest essence of things, that is the soul of all. It is the essence of Being. It is the *ātmā,* and you are like that, O Shvetaketu!"

"Please tell me more, sir."

"My child, let me continue."

Here Ends the Fourteenth *Khaṇḍa*

Fifteenth *Khaṇḍa*

Teachings to Shvetaketu Continued

1-2. "My son, consider the situation of a man who is gravely ill. His relatives gather around him and ask, 'Do you know me? Do you know me?' So long as his speech has not gone into his mind, his mind into his breath, his breath into his heat, and his heat into the highest divinity, he knows them. But once his speech has gone into his mind, his mind into his breath, his breath into his heat, and his heat into the highest divinity, he knows them not.

3. "That which is the finest essence of things, that is the soul of all. It is the essence of Being. It is the *ātmā,* and you are like that, O Shvetaketu!"

"Please tell me more, sir."

"My child, let me continue."

Here Ends the Fifteenth *Khaṇḍa*

Sixteenth *Khaṇḍa*

Teachings to Shvetaketu Continued

1-2. "My son, consider the situation of a shackled man who has been brought by people calling out, 'He has plundered! He has committed a theft! Heat the axe!' If he has committed the theft, he has made himself false. He has spoken a lie and covered himself with a lie, so let him hold the hot axe and, if he burns, execute him. On the other hand, if he is innocent and so speaks the truth, he covers himself with truth. So let him hold the hot axe and, if he does not burn, release him.

3. "What is it that keeps him from burning? It is the soul of all this world. It is the essence of Being. It is the *ātmā,* and you are like that, O Shvetaketu!"

This is what Shvetaketu learned. Indeed, Shvetaketu learned!

Here Ends the Sixteenth *Khaṇḍa*

Here Ends the Sixth *Adhyāya*

Seventh *Adhyāya*

First *Khaṇḍa*

Instructions to Narada

Name

1-2. Narada approached Sanat Kumara and said, "Good sir, teach me."

Sanat Kumara replied, "Tell me what you know and I will tell you what more there is to know."

Narada said, "I have studied the Rig, Yajur and the Sama Vedas along with the fourth Veda, the Atharva. I have also studied the fifth Veda, the histories and the Puranas. I have studied the ancestral rites, mathematics, predicting the future, chronology, dialectics and rhetoric, knowledge of the gods, rituals and spirits, knowledge of statecraft, the stars, and divine serpent beings.

3-5. Narada continued, "Good sir, I know the prayers,[1] but I do not know the *ātmā*. I have heard from the wise that knowledge of the *ātmā* releases one from sorrow. I am full of sorrow. Please, therefore, help me cross this ocean of sorrow."

---

[1] The word used here is *mantra*. The line could therefore also read "I know the mantras."

Sanat Kumara replied, "Everything you have learned is simply words.[2] The Rig, Yajur and the Sama Vedas along with the the fourth Veda, the Atharva, are all words. Even the so-called fifth Veda, the histories and the Puranas, along with the ancestral rites, mathematics, predicting the future, chronology, dialectics and rhetoric, knowledge of the gods, rituals, and spirits, knowledge of statecraft, the stars and divine serpent beings, are all words. You must, therefore, venerate words!

5. "One who understands words as *brahma* is free to go as far as words goes."[3]

"Good sir, is there anything greater than words?"

"Indeed, there is something greater than words."

"Please tell me, sir."

Here Ends the First *Khaṇḍa* of the Seventh *Adhyāya*

---

[2] The word used here is *nāma*, literally "name."

[3] Throughout *Adhyāya* 7, this is going to be a recurrent expression. This *adhyāya* is going to take us through a succession of ways, different perceptions and realizations, so to speak, to see *brahma*. Each *khaṇḍa* will end with this expression: "One who understands (insert the word) as *brahma* is free to go as far as (insert the word) goes," where the current way to see *brahma* is inserted. The point being that when one has the proper mindset, divinity is to be seen in all aspects of life.

Second *Khaṇḍa*

Instructions to Narada Continued

Speech

1. "Speech is greater than words, for speech makes all things known. Indeed, the Rig, Yajur, and the Sama Vedas, along with the fourth Veda, the Atharva, and even the so-called fifth Veda, the histories and the Puranas, along with the ancestral rites, mathematics, predicting the future, chronology, and dialectics and rhetoric, knowledge of the gods, rituals, and spirits, knowledge of statecraft, the stars and divine serpent beings are made known by speech. Indeed, even knowledge of the sky, the earth, wind, space, water, fire, the gods, human beings, domestic animals, birds, grasses, trees, and wild beasts and even worms, moths, and ants, as well as *dharma*, *adharma*, truth, falsehoods, good and evil, the pleasant and unpleasant are made known by speech. For if there were no speech, neither *dharma* or *adharma*, truth or falsehood, good or evil, pleasant or unpleasant could be known. Speech alone makes all this known. So venerate speech!

2. One who understands speech as *brahma* is free to go as far as speech can go."

"Good sir, is there anything greater than speech?"

"Indeed, there is something greater than speech."

"Please tell me, sir."

Here Ends the Second *Khaṇḍa* of the Seventh *Adhyāya*

Third *Khaṇḍa*

Instructions to Narada Continued

Mind

1. "Mind is greater than speech. As a closed fist holds two nuts, two berries, or two dice, so mind holds words and speech. When a person thinks 'I should study the mantras,' he studies. When a person thinks 'I should perform the rituals,' he performs the rituals. When a person thinks 'I should have offspring and livestock,' he seeks them. When a person thinks 'I should have this world and the afterworld,' he seeks them. For mind is the *ātmā*, mind is the world, mind is *brahma*. You should therefore venerate mind.

---

[4] *Sankalpa* is the word used here, and it has an array of meanings that cannot be fully expressed by just one word. The most common renderings are "will" and "intention," but *sankalpa* also means "mental conception," "imagination," and even "desire." Here it is said that *sankalpa* lays at the foundation of creation, that the universe itself has will, imagination and even desire. *Sankalpa* also implies consciousness, that at the most basic level of creation there is consciousness and, therefore, will, imagination and desire.

[5] Here the words are "*mantra*" and "*karma*," which may also indicate Vedic mantra formulas and ritual action; in other words, the *yajña*. But here the meaning has been generalized as "meaningful utterances" and "actions."

2. "One who understands mind as *brahma* is free to go as far as mind can go."

"Good sir, is there anything greater than mind?"

"Indeed, there is something greater than mind."

"Please tell me, sir."

Here Ends the Third *Khaṇḍa* of the Seventh *Adhyāya*

Fourth *Khaṇḍa*

Instructions to Narada Continued
Will

1. "Will[4] is greater than mind. For only by willing does a person make up his mind, and only after making up his mind does a person initiate speech and finally utter words. Utterances lead to meaningful sentences, which in turn lead to actions.[5]

2. "All these things are founded on will. Indeed, will is their very foundation and essence. The sky and earth will. Wind and space will. Water and heat will and thereby the rains will. Food results, which in turn leads to the vital breaths. And from the will of the vital breaths comes utterances and actions. This world is the will of action. Indeed, all things arise from will. Therefore, venerate will!

3. "The one who venerates will as *brahma*, becomes steadfast,

firm and fixed, and so wins these worlds that are themselves steadfast, firm and fixed. One who understands will as *brahma* is free to go as far as will can go."

"Good sir, is there anything greater than will?"

"Indeed, there is something greater than will."

"Please tell me, sir."

Here Ends the Fourth *Khaṇḍa* of the Seventh *Adhyāya*

Fifth *Khaṇḍa*

Instructions to Narada Continued

Thought

1. "Thought[6] is greater than will. For only after thought does a person have will and so make up his mind, and only after making up his mind does a person initiate speech and finally utter words. Utterances lead to meaningful sentences, which in turn lead to actions.

2. "All these things are founded on thought. Indeed, thought is their very foundation and essence. Therefore, if a person of

[6] The word is *cittam,* which means "thought," "attention," "reason," and even "intellect." Choosing the meaning is therefore highly contextual and always a little arbitrary.

[7] The word is *dhyāna*. It is usually translated as "meditation."

learning acts without thought, then people say he is useless regardless of what he knows. For if he had real knowledge, he would not be thoughtless. If, on the other hand, a person has little knowledge, but he has thought, then people listen to him. This is because all things are founded on thought. Indeed, thought is their very foundation and essence. Therefore, venerate thought.

3. "The one who venerates thought as *brahma* becomes steadfast, firm and fixed, and so wins these worlds that are themselves steadfast, firm and fixed. One who understands thought as *brahma* is free to go as far as thought can go."

"Good sir, is there anything greater than thought?"

"Indeed, there is something greater than thought."

"Please tell me, sir."

Here Ends the Fifth *Khaṇḍa* of the seventh *Adhyāya*

Sixth *Khaṇḍa*

Instructions to Narada Continued

Deep Reflection

1. "Deep reflection[7] is greater than thought. The earth is in deep reflection, as it were. The sky and the heavens are in deep reflection. The seas and the mountains are in deep reflection. The gods and men are also in deep reflection. Those who have

achieved greatness in this world have received in some measure the rewards of deep reflection. But then there are the small-minded, who are quarrelsome, niggardly, and critical in comparison to the superior ones who have received the rewards of deep reflection. Therefore, venerate deep reflection.

2. "One who venerates deep reflection as *brahma* becomes steadfast, firm and fixed, and so wins these worlds that are themselves steadfast, firm and fixed. One who understands deep reflection as *brahma* is free to go as far as deep reflection can go."

"Good sir, is there anything greater than deep reflection?"

"Indeed, there is something greater than deep reflection."

"Please tell me, sir."

Here Ends the Sixth *Khaṇḍa* of the Seventh *Adhyāya*

Seventh *Khaṇḍa*

Instructions to Narada Continued

Discernment

1. "Discernment[8] is greater than deep reflection. Indeed, the Rig, Yajur and the Sama Vedas, along with the fourth Veda, the

---

[8] The word is *vijñāna*.

Atharva, and even the so-called fifth Veda, the histories and the Puranas, along with the ancestral rites, mathematics, predicting the future, chronology, and dialectics and rhetoric, knowledge of the gods, rituals, and spirits, knowledge of statecraft, the stars and divine serpent beings are understood through discernment. Indeed, even knowledge of the sky, the earth, wind, space, water, fire, the gods, human beings, domestic animals, birds, grasses, trees, and wild beasts and even worms, moths, and ants, as well as *dharma*, *adharma*, truth, falsehoods, good and evil, the pleasant and unpleasant are understood through discernment. For if there were no discernment, neither *dharma* or *adharma*, truth or falsehood, good or evil, pleasant or unpleasant could be known. Discernment alone makes all this known. Therefore, venerate discernment!

2. "One who venerates discernment as *brahma* achieves the worlds of discernment and knowledge. He becomes steadfast, firm and fixed, and so wins these worlds that are themselves steadfast, firm and fixed. One who understands discernment as *brahma* is free to go as far as discernment can go."

"Good sir, is there anything greater than discernment?"

"Indeed, there is something greater than discernment."

"Please tell me, sir."

Here Ends the Seventh *Khaṇḍa* of the Seventh *Adhyāya*

Eighth *Khaṇḍa*

Instructions to Narada Continued

Power

1. "Indeed, power[9] is greater than discernment. One man of power makes a hundred men of discernment tremble in fear. When a man becomes powerful, he comes up in life and, as he comes up, he begins to serve and becomes a learner. On becoming educated, he becomes a seer, a hearer, and a thinker. He then becomes learned, performs good actions, and becomes wise. Because of power, the earth stands firm, the sky and the heavens are firm, and the mountains are fixed. Because of power the gods, humans, animals and birds are fixed. Out of power, the grasses, trees, wild beasts, worms, moths and ants persist. By power, the world persists. Therefore, venerate power.

2. "One who venerates power as *brahma* becomes steadfast, firm and fixed, and so wins these worlds that are themselves steadfast, firm and fixed. One who understands power as *brahma* is free to go as far as power can go."

"Good Sir, is there anything greater than power?"

"Indeed, there is something greater than power."

---

[9] The word is *bala*.

"Please tell me, sir."

Here Ends the Eighth *Khaṇḍa* of the Seventh *Adhyāya*

Ninth *Khaṇḍa*

Instructions to Narada Continued

Food

1. "Food, indeed, is greater than power. If one fails to eat for ten days, even though he continues to live, he will not be able to see, hear, think, understand, act or comprehend. Yet, once he eats, he will see, hear, think, understand, act and comprehend once again. Therefore, venerate food.

2. "One who understands food as *brahma* wins the worlds of food and drink. He becomes steadfast, firm and fixed, and so wins these worlds that are themselves steadfast, firm and fixed. One who understands food as *brahma* is free to go as far as food can go."

"Good sir, is there anything greater than food?"

"Indeed, there is something greater than food."

"Please tell me, sir."

Here Ends the Ninth *Khaṇḍa* of the Seventh *Adhyāya*

Tenth *Khaṇḍa*

Instructions to Narada Continued

Water

1. "Water, indeed, is greater than food. When the rains diminish, all creatures worry and think food will be less.' But when rains are plentiful, they become joyful and think 'Food will be in plenty!' In fact, all things—the earth, the sky, the heavens, the mountains, the gods, men, domestic animals, birds, grasses, trees, wild beasts and even worms, moths and ants—are just forms of water. Therefore, venerate water.

2. "One who understands water as *brahma* obtains all his desires and becomes satisfied. He becomes steadfast, firm and fixed, and so wins these worlds that are themselves steadfast, firm and fixed. One who understands water as *brahma* is free to go as far as water can go."

"Good sir, is there anything greater than water?"

"Indeed, there is something greater than water."

"Please tell me, sir."

Here Ends the Tenth *Khaṇḍa* of the Seventh *Adhyāya*

Eleventh *Khaṇḍa*

Instructions to Narada Continued

Heat

1. "Heat, indeed, is greater than water. Heat first blocks the wind and then heats everything. People say 'It's burning, it's a scorcher, it will rain!' First the heat comes, and then the rains come. Lightning streaks upward and across the sky, and then thunder rolls across the land, and so they say 'Lightning is flashing. Thunder is rolling. It will rain!' Therefore, first heat comes and then rains arrive. Therefore, venerate heat.

2. "One who understands heat as *brahma* becomes radiant and comes to possess the worlds full of radiance, full of light, and free of darkness. One who understands heat as *brahma* is free to go as far as heat can go."

"Good sir, is there anything greater than heat?"

"Indeed, there is something greater than heat."

"Please tell that to me, sir."

Here Ends the Eleventh *Khaṇḍa* of the Seventh *Adhyāya*

Twelfth *Khaṇḍa*

Instructions to Narada Continued

Space

1. "Space,[10] indeed, is greater than heat. Both the sun and the moon exist within space. Lightning, the constellations and fire exist in space. One calls out through space. One hears and answers back across space. One enjoys and suffers within space. One is born into space and one lives within space. Therefore, venerate space.

2. "One who understands space as *brahma* himself becomes spacious and wins worlds that are spacious, shining, and unbounded. One who understands space as *brahma* is free to go as far as space can go."

"Good sir, is there anything greater than space?"

"Indeed, there is something greater than space."

"Please tell that to me, sir."

Here Ends the Twelfth *Khaṇḍa* of the Seventh *Adhyāya*

---

[10] The word is *ākāśa.*

[11] The word is *smara.*

[12] The word is *āśā.*

[13] The words used here are *mantra* and *karma*, which are commonly interpreted to mean Vedic chants and rituals. Here the words have been rendered in a more universal way.

Thirteenth *Khaṇḍa*

Instructions to Narada Continued

Memory

1. "Memory,[11] indeed, is greater than space. If people come together, yet they have no memory, they would not be able to hear, think, or recognize anything. When they have memory, they can hear, think, and recognize. It is through memory that a man knows his sons and animals. Therefore, venerate memory.

2. "One who understands memory as *brahma* is free to go as far as memory can go."

"Good sir, is there anything greater than memory?"

"Indeed, there is something greater than memory."

"Please tell that to me, sir."

Here Ends the Thirteenth *Khaṇḍa* of the Seventh *Adhyāya*

Fourteenth *Khaṇḍa*

Instructions to Narada Continued

Hope

1. "Hope,[12] indeed, is greater than memory. Kindled by hope, a person with memory learns language and performs actions,[13] desires sons and animals, and seeks this world and the next.

Therefore, venerate hope.

2. "One who understands hope as *brahma,* with hope alone all his desires and prayers can be fulfilled and he is free to go as far as hope can go."

"Good sir, is there anything greater than hope?"

"Indeed, there is something greater than hope."

"Please tell that to me, sir."

Here Ends the Fourteenth *Khaṇḍa* of the Seventh *Adhyāya*

Fifteenth *Khaṇḍa*

Instructions to Narada Continued

Breath

1. "Breath,[14] indeed, is greater than hope. As spokes on a wheel are connected to the hub, all things are connected to breath. Because of breath, life goes on. Breath gives to breath. Breath exists for breath. A father is breath. A mother is breath. A brother and a sister are breath. The teacher and the *brāhmaṇa* are breath.

2-4. "If someone speaks harshly to a father, mother, brother or a sister, or to a teacher or a *brāhmaṇa,* people chastise that person, saying 'You harm your father; you harm your mother; you

[14] The word is *prāṇa*.

harm your brother; you harm your sister; you harm your teacher; and you harm the *brāhmaṇa.*' But when all these breaths have departed, their bodies are pushed into the funeral fire with a poker and completely burned, and no one says 'You are a father killer; you are a mother killer; you are a brother or sister killer; you are a teacher or *brāhmaṇa* killer.' For it is only breath that has become all these things. A person who sees and thinks and understands this becomes outspoken about this. And when people say, 'You talk too much about this; you should not deny it, but simply acknowledge,' the person who sees and thinks and understands this replies, 'Yes, I am outspoken about this."

Here Ends the Fifteenth *Khaṇḍa* of the Seventh *Adhyāya*

Sixteenth *Khaṇḍa*

Instructions to Narada Continued

Outspoken for the Truth

1. Sanat Kumara said, "An outspoken person should be outspoken for the truth."

Narada replied, "Good sir, I wish to be outspoken for the truth."

"Then you must desire to know the truth!"

"Good sir, I desire to know the truth."

Here Ends the Sixteenth *Khaṇḍa* of the Seventh *Adhyāya*

Seventeenth *Khaṇḍa*

Instructions to Narada Continued

Discernment

1. "When a man knows the truth, he speaks the truth. When he does not know the truth, he does not speak the truth. Let him, therefore, know the truth and speak the truth. Indeed, he should cultivate discernment to know the truth."

"Good sir, I desire to know discernment."

Here Ends the Seventeenth *Khaṇḍa* of the Seventh *Adhyāya*

Eighteenth *Khaṇḍa*

Instructions to Narada Continued

Thinking

1. "Only when a man thinks can he know. But if he does not think, he will never know. So let him desire to think."[15]

"Good sir, I desire to think!"

Here Ends the Eighteenth *Khaṇḍa* of the Seventh *Adhyāya*

---

[15] The word is *mati*.

[16] The word is *śraddhā.* Faith has been defined as *āstikya-buddhi.*

[17] Here the word is *niṣṭhā.*

Nineteenth *Khaṇḍa*

Instructions to Narada Continued

Faith

1. "Only when a man has faith[16] does he think. Without faith, he does not think. Therefore, let him have faith and let him think. You should desire to know faith."

"Good sir, I do desire to know faith!"

Here Ends the Nineteenth *Khaṇḍa* of the Seventh *Adhyāya*

Twentieth *Khaṇḍa*

Instructions to Narada Continued

Resolve

1. "A man first must stand firm. Then he will have faith. Without resolve, he will not have faith. Let him, therefore, have resolve[17] and then let him have faith. You should desire to know resolve."

"Good sir, I do desire to know resolve!"

Here Ends the Twentieth *Khaṇḍa* of the Seventh *Adhyāya*

Twenty-first *Khaṇḍa*

Instructions to Narada Continued

Action

1. "A man first must act. Then he finds resolve. Without acting, he does not have resolve. Therefore, let him have action[18] and then let him know resolve. You should desire to know action."

"Good sir, I do desire to know action!"

Here Ends the Twenty-first *Khaṇḍa* of the Seventh *Adhyāya*

Twenty-second *Khaṇḍa*

Instructions to Narada Continued

Happiness

1. "A man first must obtain happiness[19] before he acts. Without happiness, one does not act. Therefore, let him obtain happiness and then let him act. You should desire to know happiness."

---

[18] The word is *kṛti.*

[19] The word is *sukha.*

[20] The two words used in this section, "abundance" and "scarcity," are, respectively, *bhūman* and *alpa*. The word *bhūman* means wealth, plenty, and opulence. The word *alpa* means small, little, and scanty. *Apla* contrasts with *bhūman*, and commentators often translate the two as "the infinite" and "the finite."

"Good sir, I do desire to know happiness!"

Here Ends the Twenty-second *Khaṇḍa* of the Seventh *Adhyāya*

Twenty-third *Khaṇḍa*

Instructions to Narada Continued
Abundance

1. "Happiness is based on abundance. When there is scarcity, there can be no happiness.[20] Therefore happiness is found in abundance. You should desire to know abundance."

"Good sir, I do desire to know abundance!"

Here Ends the Twenty-third *Khaṇḍa* of the Seventh *Adhyāya*

Twenty-fourth *Khaṇḍa*

Instructions to Narada Continued
Abundance and Scarcity

1. "Abundance is where a man sees, hears and knows only one thing. Scarcity is where a man sees, hears and knows other things. Abundance is the immortal. Scarcity is the mortal."

"Good sir, on what is abundance based?"

"On its own greatness, or perhaps not.[21]

2. "In this world cows and horses, elephants and gold, servants and wives, farms and homes are what people consider abundance. But I do not agree. Instead, I say these things are all based on each other."[22]

Here Ends the Twenty-fourth *Khaṇḍa* of the Seventh *Adhyāya*

Twenty-fifth *Khaṇḍa*

Instructions to Narada Continued

Abundance is all Around

1. "Abundance is below, abundance is above; abundance is in the west, the east, the south and the north. Indeed, abundance is throughout this world.

"Now this instruction in terms of 'I': I am below, I am above, I am in the west, I am in the east, I am in the south and I am in

[21] This last part is a suggestion of doubt, and it is reminiscent of the doubts about creation expressed in the RV 10.129 *nāsadīya* hymn. The tendency for scripture to self-doubt is one of the greatest features of early Hinduism.

[22] For example, the concept of "high" is dependent on "low." "Happiness" depends on there being "unhappiness." In other words, the so-called abundance of this world is actually scarcity. It is relative.

[23] This is generally translated as mantras and Vedic ritual action. Here it is generalized.

the north. Indeed, I exist throughout this world.

2. "Now this instruction in terms of '*ātmā*:' The *ātmā* is below, the *ātmā* is above; the *ātmā* is in the west, the *ātmā* is in the east, the *ātmā* is in the south and the *ātmā* is in the north. Indeed, the *ātmā* exists throughout this world.

"A person who truly sees this, who thinks this, who knows this, who takes pleasure in the *ātmā*, who plays with the *ātmā*, who has union with the *ātmā*, and who finds joy in the *ātmā* becomes his own master. He has complete freedom to move throughout all the worlds. But those who think otherwise become dependent on others and obtain only these perishable worlds; they have only limited movement in these worlds."

Here Ends the Twenty-fifth *Khaṇḍa* of the Seventh *Adhyāya*

Twenty-sixth *Khaṇḍa*

Instructions to Narada End

1. "When a person sees in this way, thinks in this way and understands in this way, he knows that breath and hope, memory and space, heat and water, appearance and disappearance, food and strength, and even understanding and meditation all arise from the *ātmā*. Similarly, he knows that thought and reason, intention and mind, speech and name, words and actions[23] also spring from the *ātmā*. Indeed, this whole world springs from the *ātmā*.

2. "In this regard there is the following verse:

A seer sees no death, no disease and no suffering.
A seer sees all things and obtains all things.
He is one. He is three and five and seven and nine and eleven.
He is a hundred and eleven. He is twenty thousand.[24]

"With pure food one's existence becomes pure. When one's existence is pure, the memory becomes strong. When one's memory is strong, all the knots in the heart are loosened. To such a person, whose stains are removed, Lord Sanat Kumara points the way beyond darkness. They call him learned.[25] He, indeed, is truly learned."

Here Ends the twenty-sixth *Khaṇḍa*
Here Ends the Seventh *Adhyāya*

---

[24] These number references are obscure.

[25] The word is *skanda*, which means learned. Such a person is learned.

Eighth *Adhyāya*

First *Khaṇḍa*

The City of *Brahma*

1. There is a city of *brahma,*[1] and in this city there is a small lotus, the abode,[2] and within this abode there is a private space that one should try to find and try to know.

2. Now if they ask, "So in this city of *brahma*, with its small lotus abode and its private space, what is it that should be found and what is it that should be known?" he should answer:

3. "As space in the outside world extends everywhere, so space within the heart extends everywhere. Both heaven and earth exist within each space.[3]

"Both fire and wind, sun and moon, lightning and the constellations exist within each space. Whatever he possesses and whatever he does not, exists within each space."

---

[1] The body is the city of *brahma.*

[2] The heart.

[3] This is a common theme throughout the Upanishads, that there is a matching relationship between the inside world and the outside world. The individual is the universe in miniature. Whatever exists in the universe also exists within the individual. This is the basis of Hindu architecture and even astronomy and astrology. It is said, as above, so below.

4. And if they further ask, "So in this city of *brahma,* if the whole world, along with all its beings and all their desires, is contained within, what is it that is left when old age comes and a man perishes?"

5. To this he should answer,

"It does not age when the body ages;
It is not killed when the body is killed.
This is the true city of *brahma*,
Wherein all desires are contained.

"This *ātmā* is free of evil: it never ages, it is immortal; it experiences no sorrow, no hunger, no thirst, and its intentions and desires always come true. In this world, beings possess things according to law; so whatever they desire, be it a kingdom or just a plot of land, they live with it and come to depend on it.

---

[4] "Acquired by merit" is *puṇya-jita.* The idea of merit is that good deeds performed in this world lead to merit that accumulates and ultimately gives rise to a good position in a future life.

[5] This chapter involves phrase repetition. In this first instance the expression is *pitṛ-loka-kāma*. The next instances are *mātṛ-loka-kāma* and then *bhrātṛ-loka-kāma*, etc., Literally, it means desire for the world of father, the world of mother, the world of brother, and so on. The translation "appear" is *samuttiṣṭhanti*, which is literally "they stand up." The translation "intention" is *saṅkalpa,* which has shades of meaning: mental resolve, will, or determination.

6. "But whatever is acquired by work in this world perishes, and whatever is acquired by merit in the next world also perishes.[4] So those who depart this world without knowing the *ātmā* and their true self-interest lose their freedom to move in these worlds, but those who come to know the *ātmā* and their true self-interest gain full independence in all these worlds."

Here ends the First *Khaṇḍa*

Second *Khaṇḍa*

The Object of Desire

1-9. If a person desires fatherhood, fatherhood appears due to that intention; and having attained fatherhood, that person is happy.[5]

2. If a person desires motherhood, motherhood appears due to that intention; and having attained motherhood, that person is happy.

3. If a person desires brotherhood, brotherhood appears due to that intention; and having attained brotherhood, that person is happy.

4. If a person desires sisterhood, sisterhood appears due to that intention; and having attained sisterhood, that person is happy.

5. If a person desires friendship, friendship appears due to that intention; and having attained friendship, that person is happy.

6. If a person desires fragrances and garlands, fragrances and garlands appear due to that intention; and having gained fragrances and garlands, that person is happy.

7. If a person desires food and drink, food and drink appear due to that intention; and having gained food and drink, that person is happy.

8. If a person desires singing and music, singing and music appear due to that intention; and having gained singing and music, that person is happy.

9. If a person desires women, women draw close to him due to that intention; and having gained women, that person is happy.

10. Whatever is the object of one's desire, anything at all, that object appears due to that intention; and having attained one's desire, that person is happy.

---

[6] The word is *anṛta. Ṛta* is what is true, proper and honest. *An-ṛta* is what is untrue, improper and dishonest. Here it is stated that true desires are covered by something which is untrue.

[7] The small abode in the city of *brahma.* See CU 8.1.1.

[8] This would seem to be a likely source of the later Vedanta theory of *māyā*, illusion.

[9] Here the word *hṛdaya* is dissolved into *hṛdi ayam:* "in the heart, this."

[10] Literally, "goes to heaven every day." During deep sleep, a person who realizes this enters that *brahma* in the heart. This is considered a heaven.

Here Ends the Second *Khaṇḍa*

Third *Khaṇḍa*

True Desires

1. These are all true desires, though they have been covered by what is false.[6] It is like a friend who has departed this world and can no longer be seen.

2. On the other hand, friends, living or not, or other desirable things that cannot be obtained, can indeed be found by entering into that place;[7] for in that place, true desires, which have been covered by the unreal, can be found.

When a treasure of gold lays hidden in the ground, people, who do not know, walk over it every day and never find it. Similarly, all beings move through this world and never see the world of *brahma*. This is because it is hidden by the unreal.[8]

3. This *ātmā* is located within the heart (*hṛdaya*); hence the etymology of the word *hṛdaya.*[9] One who knows this resides always in heaven.[10]

4. And so this blessed one rises up from the body and emerges in all radiance in his true form. He declares, "This is the *ātmā* . It is immortal. It is devoid of fear. It is *brahma.* Its name is *satya*, truth."

5. *Satya* is composed of three syllables, *sa, ti,* and *ya,* where *sa*

is the immortal, *ti* is the mortal, and *ya* is what brings the two together.[11] Because it joins the two, it is called *ya*. One who knows this goes to heaven every day.

Here ends the Third *Khaṇḍa*

Fourth *Khaṇḍa*

The *Ātmā* as a Bridge

1. This *ātmā* is a bridge that separates two worlds. Across this bridge there is no day or night, no old age or death, no sorrow, or even good or bad deeds. All evil is turned away. This realm of *brahma* is free of evil.

2. As one crosses this bridge, if one is blind, blindness is removed. If one is wounded, wounds are healed. If one is sick,

---

[11] Here both worlds are interrelated. Both the immortal and the mortal are real.

[12] Here two words are used, *yajña* and *brahmacarya*. *Yajña* means sacrifice, which is commonly used in the Upanishads to refer to the Vedic fire sacrifice, the *agni-hotra*. Here *yajña* is used in the sense of giving up something to obtain something higher, which here is the path of *brahmacarya*, the disciplined life of a student of sacred knowledge. The word *brahmacarya* is comprised of two parts, *brahma* and *carya*. The word *carya* means a way or path. So *brahmacarya* is literally the way to *brahma*. In tradition there is a word *brahmacarin,* which is one of the four stages of life, which involves living at the house of a teacher, study of the Vedas, and practicing chastity.

[13] Here the word is *sattrāyana*, which refers to a particular elaborate and grand Vedic fire ritual.

sickness is removed. There is no nighttime, only daytime, because this world of *brahma* always shines with its own light.

3. This is the realm of *brahma* found by the students of *brahma,* wherein they walk with complete freedom in all these worlds.

Here Ends the Fourth *Khaṇḍa*

Fifth *Khaṇḍa*

Brahmacarya

1. Now, what people call sacrifice is in fact *brahmacarya*, the disciplined life of a student of sacred knowledge,[12] for it is only by *brahmacarya* that a learned man finds *brahma.*

Now, what people call "sacrifice" is in fact *brahmacarya.* For it is only by seeking, through *brahmacarya* that one finds the *ātmā*.

2. Now, what people call a major sacrifice[13] is in fact *brahmacarya.* For it is only by *brahmacarya* that one finds protection for the true *ātmā.*

Now, what people call a vow of silence is in fact *brahmacarya.* For it is only by *brahmacarya* that one finds the *ātmā* and then meditates on it.

3. Now, what people call fasting is in fact *brahmacarya,* for the *ātmā* that one finds by *brahmacarya* is never destroyed.

Now, what people call going to the wilderness is in fact *brahma-carya.* Ara and Nya are two seas in the world of *brahma.* They are in the third heaven from here.[14] In that world there is a lake known as Airammadiya, a banyan tree known as Somasavana, a fort known as Aparajita, and a golden palace known as Prabhu.

4. So it is only by *brahmacarya* that one finds these two seas, Ara and Nya, in the world of *brahma*. Those who practice *brahmacarya,* they alone possess this *brahma* world and have complete freedom to move throughout all these worlds.

Here ends the Fifth *Khaṇḍa*

Sixth *Khaṇḍa*

The Pathways of the Heart

1. The pathways[15] of the heart are extremely fine and multicolored: orange, white, blue, yellow and red. The sun is similarly multicolored: orange, white, blue, yellow and red.

---

[14] In the later puranic model of the universe, there are three heavens above earth called *svargas* and three hells below earth known as *narakas*. This makes a total of seven levels or *lokas*, three *lokas* up and three *lokas* down with the earth in the middle. The topmost heaven is called *brahma-loka*. This verse seems to be a description of the geography of *brahma-loka.*

[15] The word is *nāḍī*, which means a tube, a vein, or an artery.

[16] The word is *raśmi*, which means a ray.

2. As a main road runs between two villages, going from this village to that distant village, so the rays[16] of the sun extend between both worlds, this one here and that one up there. They extend from the sun up there and slip into these pathways of the heart, and then again from these pathways and into the rays of the sun.

3. A soundly sleeping person is calm and serene and experiences no dreams because he has entered into these pathways within the heart. No evils can touch him at this time for he is bathed in radiance.

4-5. When a person has become weak and infirm, friends and relatives gather around him and say, "Do you know me? Do you know me?" As long as he remains within the body, he knows them; but once he begins to depart, he rises up through one of these pathways and leaves reciting the sound *om*.

In an instant he goes to the sun. This is the gateway the learned take to the higher worlds, but not the ignorant.

6. In this regard there is the following verse:

A hundred and one pathways emanate from the heart.
One of these pierces the crown of the head.
Traveling along this pathway one reaches immortality.
Other pathways reach other destinations.

Here Ends the Sixth *Khaṇḍa*

Seventh *Khaṇḍa*

The *Ātmā* Seen in the Eye

1. This *ātmā* is free of evil. It never becomes old and dies. It is free of sorrow, hunger and thirst, and its desires and intentions are true. This *ātmā* should be sought and known. When a person discovers and understands this *ātmā,* he gains access to all these worlds and all his desires are fulfilled. So said the Lord of Creatures, Prajapati!

2. When the gods and the demons[17] came to know of this, they separately spoke amongst themselves. "We should seek that *ātmā* so that we may conquer all these worlds and fulfill our desires." Thus Indra, for the gods, and Virocana, for the demons, set out without knowing the other's intention. With fuel in hand, they both arrived at the home of the Lord of Creatures, Prajapati.

3. For thirty-two years they lived as celibate students, and finally Prajapati spoke to them: "Why have you stayed here? What do you want?"

They replied, "Good sir, people say that you have said, 'This *ātmā* is free of evil. It never becomes old and dies. It is free of sorrow, hunger and thirst, and its desires and intentions are true. This *ātmā* should be sought and known. When a person dis-

---

[17] Both the gods and the demons are the children of Prajapati.

covers and understands this *ātmā,* he gains access to all these worlds and all his desires are fulfilled.' This *ātmā* is what we seek, Good sir."

4. Prajapati spoke to them, "The person you see in the eye is the *ātmā*. He is immortal. He is without fear. He is *brahma.*"

They both then asked, "But the one perceived in water or in a mirror, who is that, Good sir?"

"The same one perceived in both cases," Prajapati replied.

Here Ends the Seventh *Khaṇḍa*

Eighth *Khaṇḍa*

The *Ātmā* as the Body

1. Prajapati said, "Look into this container of water and tell me what you see."

They both looked into the water and said, "Good sir, we see ourselves, complete, right down to our hair and nails."

2. Prajapati again said to them, "Go and dress and adorn yourselves. Then return and look into the water." They went and dressed and adorned themselves and returned. They looked into the water. Prajapati said, "Tell me what you see."

3. They replied, "Good sir, we see our reflection nicely dressed

and adorned, just as we are."

Prajapati replied, "This is the *ātmā*, immortal and fearless. It is *brahma*." They both went away with hearts satisfied.

4. As Prajapati watched them leaving, he thought, "They leave without perceiving or knowing the *ātmā*. If they adhere to this teaching they will be vanquished."

Virocana happily returned to the *asuras* and gave them this teaching: It is the body that one should make happy and attend to. A person who makes the body happy and attends to the body obtains both this world and the next world.

5. Therefore, even today they say of a person who is without a charitable sprit, who is faithless and who does not sacrifice, "Alas, he is an *asura*!" *Asuras* follow this doctrine and so they perform the funerary rites for the body of a deceased person with food and garments and ornaments thinking that by doing so they will gain the next world.

Here Ends the Eighth *Khaṇḍa*

Ninth *Khaṇḍa*

The *Ātmā* as the Body (continued)

1. As Indra was approaching the devas, he saw this danger: If this body is the *ātmā*, then, when the body is nicely dressed, ornamented and adorned, then the *ātmā* is nicely dressed, orna-

mented and adorned. But when the body has become blind, lame and disfigured, the *ātmā* will be blind, lame and disfigured. This means when the body perishes, the *ātmā* perishes. I see no pleasure in this.

2. So with wood in hand, Indra returned. Prajapati said to him, "Indra, you left here with Virocana. So why have you returned?"

Indra replied, "If this body is the *ātmā,* then when the body is nicely dressed, ornamented and adorned, then the *ātmā* is nicely dressed, ornamented, and adorned. But when the body has become blind, lame and disfigured, the *ātmā* will be blind, lame and disfigured. This means when the body perishes, the *ātmā* also perishes. I see no pleasure in this."

3. Prajapati replied, "Yes! What you say is true. Remain here another thirty-two years and I will tell you more." Indra remained another thirty-two years, and then Prajapati spoke to him once again.

Here Ends the Ninth *Khaṇḍa*

Tenth *Khaṇḍa*

The Dreamer as the *Ātmā*

1-2. Prajapati spoke: "The one who moves about happily in dreams, he is the *ātmā.* He is immortal, he is without fear, he is *brahma.*" Indra then departed happily, but, as he approached the devas, he saw this danger: "It is true that when the body becomes blind or lame, this *ātmā* does not become blind or lame. It is true that this *ātmā* does not suffer the faults of the body. It is not killed when the body is killed. It does not become lame when the body becomes lame. But in dreams it can be killed, in dreams it is chased and experiences unpleasant things. It even cries! I do not see any pleasure in this."

3. Fuel in hand, he returned, and Prajapati spoke to him. "Indra, you left here contented, but you have returned. What is it that you desire?"

Indra said, "It is true that when the body becomes blind or lame, this *ātmā* does not become blind or lame. It is true that this *ātmā* does not suffer the faults of the body. It is not killed when the body is killed. It does not become lame when the body becomes lame. But in dreams it can be killed, in dreams it is chased and experiences unpleasant things. It even cries! I do not see any pleasure in this."

Prajapati said, "Yes! What you say is true. Remain here for another thirty-two years and I will tell you more." Indra remained for another thirty-two years. Then Prajapati spoke to him once again.

Here Ends the Tenth *Khaṇḍa*

Eleventh *Khaṇḍa*

The Deep Sleeper as the *Ātmā*

1. Prajapati spoke: "The one who is in deep sleep, contented and without dreams, he is the *ātmā.* He is immortal, he is without fear, he is *brahma.*" Indra then departed happily, but, as he approached the devas, he saw this danger: "Indeed, this *ātmā* thus explained does not even know 'I am this,' nor does he know the existence of other beings. It has become completely annihilated, as it were. I do not see any pleasure in this."

2. Fuel in hand, he returned, and Prajapati spoke to him: "Indra, you left contented, but you have returned. What is it that you desire?"

Indra spoke: "Indeed, this *ātmā* you have explained does not even know 'I am this,' nor does he know the existence of other beings. Good sir, it has become completely annihilated, as it were. I do not see any pleasure in this."

3. Prajapati replied, "Yes, Indra, what you say is true. Remain here another five years and I will tell you more." Indra remained for five more years. Altogether this makes one hundred and one years, which is why people say "Indra lived as a celibate student with Prajapati for one hundred and one years." Prajapati then spoke to him.

Here Ends the Eleventh *Khaṇḍa*

Twelfth *Khaṇḍa*

The Pleasures of the *Ātmā*

1. "This mortal body, even though it is the resting place for the immortal, bodiless *ātmā,* has been given over to death. One who has a body, O Indra, must accept what is both pleasing and unpleasing. Indeed, for one embodied there is no way to avoid pleasure or pain. On the other hand, one without a body is never touched by pleasure or pain.

2-3. "The wind is bodiless. Clouds, lightning and thunder are bodiless; and as they rise up from this earthly realm and reach the light of the sky, they take on their natural form. So this serene one, the *ātmā*, rises up from this body and reaches the supreme light and assumes its natural form. He is the highest person, and in his natural form he moves about, laughing, playing, and enjoying with women, vehicles, and relations without remembering his former body. As a horse is bound to its cart, so this life force is bound to this body.

---

[18] The words here are *śyāma* and *śabala*, literally "dark" and "multicolored." Ś*yāma* and *śabala* are also the two dogs of Yama, the god of death, and they generally mean the moon and the sun. This seems to be a suggestion of the rotation of the soul through this world life after life.

[19] In Hindu mythology a lunar eclipse occurs when the moon is swallowed by the head of a demon named *rāhu*.

[20] This is written as a prayer to be recited.

4-5. "Sight arises when the person owning the eye and the eye itself gaze out into space. Similarly, when the *ātmā* desires 'Let me smell,' the faculty of smell arises. When the *ātmā* desires 'Let me speak,' speech arises. When the *ātmā* desires 'Let me hear,' the faculty of hearing arises. When the *ātmā* desires 'Let me think,' the divine faculty of seeing in the mind arises. Indeed, with this divine sight the embodied soul sees the pleasures in *brahma's* world and so enjoys.

6. "For this reason the gods venerate the *ātmā* and so have gained these worlds and have fulfilled their desires. Similarly, when a person perceives the *ātmā* and comes to understand, he too obtains these worlds and has his desires fulfilled." Thus spoke Prajapati!

Here Ends the Twelfth *Khaṇḍa*

Thirteenth *Khaṇḍa*

A Prayer of Release from this World

1. From darkness to light, from light to darkness, I go.[18] As a horse shakes dust from its hair, may I become freed from evil. Like the moon freed from the jaws of darkness,[19] may my perfected soul cast off this soiled body and attain to the world of *brahma*.[20]

Here Ends the Thirteenth *Khaṇḍa*

Fourteenth *Khaṇḍa*

A Prayer to Glory

1. Name and form arise from space. They exist within *brahma.* That is the immortal. It is the *ātmā*. I enter the abode and assembly of Prajapati, the Lord of Creatures. I am the glory of priests (the *brāhmaṇas*). I am the glory of kings, I am the glory of traders. I have attained glory! I am the glory of glories! May I never become grey, toothless and slobbery. Yea, may I never become grey, toothless and slobbery!

Here Ends the Fourteenth *Khaṇḍa*

Fifteenth *Khaṇḍa*

The Conclusion

1. Brahmā spoke this knowledge to Prajapati. Prajapati in turn spoke it to Manu, and Manu taught it to mankind. A person who has learned the Vedas from a teacher in the proper way, who has fulfilled his obligation to his teacher, who has returned to a clean and sanctified home, who studies and teaches sons and disciples, who focuses his senses on the *ātmā*, who harms no beings except as permitted in scripture, that person reaches the world of *brahma,* never to return to this world. Yea, that person never returns to this world!

Here Ends the Fifteenth *Khaṇḍa*
Here Ends the Eighth *Adhyāya*

Here Ends the *Chandogya* Upanishad

Sanskrit Glossary

ācārya–traditional teacher or theologian of Hindu doctrine, head of *sampradāya* or school of religious thought.

adharma–the opposite of *dharma*. The term is often used in the sense of unrighteousness, impiety or non-performance of duty.

adhibhūta–the manifestation of *brahma* as the perishable nature of matter.

adhidaiva–the manifestation of *brahma* as the Universal Person or *puruṣa* who is the foundation of the gods.

adhiyajña–the principle of divinity that dwells within all things and is the recipient of all sacrifice.

adhyātmā–the manifestation of *brahma* as the individual soul.

advaita–non dualism, the name given to the theological position of the Shankara school of thought.

agni–fire or the fire deity.

ahimsā–nonviolence.

akṣara–something that is imperishable, the soul, God.

āryan–one of noble birth, one faithful to the religion of the Vedas.

artha–wealth, not to be understood solely as material assets, but all kinds of wealth including non-tangibles such as knowledge, friendship and love. *Artha* is one of the four *puruṣārthas* or "goals of life," the others being *dharma*, *kāma* and *mokṣa*.

āśrama–one of the four stages of life: *brahmacarya* (studentship), *gārhasthya* (householder), *vānaprastha* (retired), and *sannyāsa* (renounced); a hermitage.

asat–opposite of *sat,* non-being, impermanent, false, evil, unreal, some- times used to refer to matter or to the body.

asura–an ungodly one, a demon, one who does not follow the path of the Vedas.

ātman–has many meanings in Sanskrit that include: soul, breath, the Self, one's self (as a reflexive pronoun), mind, body, the Supreme Soul, etc.

avatāra–literally, one who descends, an incarnation of God who descends into this physical world, an incarnation of Viṣṇu.

avidyā–non knowledge, ignorance, nescience.

bhagavān–literally, one possessed of *bhaga*. *Bhaga* means fame, glory, strength, power, etc. The word is used as an epithet applied to God, gods, or any holy or venerable personality.

bhakta–a devotee, one who follows the path of devotion.

bhakti–love, devotion. One of the most common forms of *yoga*.

bhakti-yoga–the spiritual path of connecting one's self to God through devotion.

brahmā–the four headed creator god born of the lotus.

brahmacārī–a religious student in the first stage of life.

brahmacarya–the first stage of life, studentship, celibacy.

brahman–derived from the Sanskrit root *bṛmh* meaning to grow, to expand, to bellow, to roar. The word *brahman* refers to the Supreme Principle regarded as impersonal and divested of all qualities. *Brahman* is the essence from which all created beings are produced and into which they are absorbed. This word is neuter and not to be confused with the masculine word Brahmā, the creator god. *Brahman* is sometimes used to denote the syllable *om* or the *Vedas* in general.

brāhmaṇa–a member of the traditional priestly class. The *brāhmaṇa* was the first of the four *varṇas* in the social system called *varṇāśrama- dharma*. Literally, the word means "in relation to brahman." A *brāhmaṇa* is one who follows the ways of *brahman*. Traditionally a *brāhmaṇa*, often written as brahmin, filled the role of priest, teacher and thinker.

candra–the moon or the moon deity.

deva–derived from the Sanskrit root *div* meaning to shine or become bright. A *deva* is therefore a "shining one." The word is used to refer to God, a god or any exalted personality. The female version is *devī*.

devanāgarī–name of the writing script in which Sanskrit and Hindi are usually written.

dharma–derived from the Sanskrit root *dhṛ* meaning to hold up, to carry, to bear, to sustain. The word *dharma* refers to that which upholds or sustains the universe. Human society, for example, is sustained and upheld by the *dharma* performed by its members. Parents protecting and maintaining children, children being obedient to parents, the king protecting the citizens are acts of *dharma* that uphold and sustain society. In this context *dharma* has the meaning of duty. *Dharma* also employs the meaning of law, religion, virtue, and ethics. These things uphold and sustain the proper functioning of human society. In philosophy *dharma* refers to the defining quality of an object. For instance, liquidity is one of the essential *dharmas* of water; coldness is a *dharma* of ice. In this case we can think that the existence of an object is sustained or defined by its essential attributes, *dharmas*.

duḥkha–suffering or unhappiness.

dvaita–dualism, the name given to the theological position of the Mādhva school of thought.

dvāpara-yuga–the third time period (*yuga*) said to last 864,000 years (two times 432,000)

gaṅgā–the river Ganges.

gārhasthya–the third order (*āśrama*) of life, domestic affairs.

gāyatrī–a meter used throughout the Vedas comprised of three lines of eight measures totaling twenty-four measures. A sacred chant.

guṇa–quality, positive attributes or virtues. In the context of *Bhagavad* Gītā and *Sāṅkhya* philosophy there are three *guṇas* of matter. Sometimes *guṇa* is translated as phase or mode. Therefore the three *guṇas* or phases of matter are: *sattva-guṇa*, *rajo-guṇa* and *tamo- guṇa*. The word *guṇa* also means a rope or thread and it is sometimes said that beings are "roped" or "tied" into matter by the three *guṇas* of material nature.

gṛhastha–one situated in the second order of life (*āśrama*), a householder.

guru–a teacher. Literally, the word means heavy and so refers to one "heavy" with knowledge, commonly used to refer to a spiritual teacher.

haṭha-yoga–a path of physical discipline meant to control the senses.

Īśā–literally, lord, master, or controller. *Īśā* is one of the words used for God as the supreme controller. The word is also used to refer to any being or personality who is in control.

Īśvara–see Īśā.

japa–chanting.

jīva–the soul, a living being.

jñāna–derived from the Sanskrit root *jñā*, to know, to learn, to experience. In the context of *Bhagavad Gītā* and the *Upaniṣads*, *jñāna* is generally used in the sense of spiritual knowledge or awareness.

jñāna-yoga–the spiritual path of connecting one's self to God through knowledge.

jñānī–literally, "one possessed of knowledge," a scholar.

kāma–wish, desire, love. Often used in the sense of sexual desire or love, but not necessarily. *Kāma* is one of the four *puruṣārthas* or "goals of life," the others being *dharma, artha* and *mokṣa.*

kāla–time.

kali-yuga–one of the four ages, said to last 432,000 years, the age characterized by fighting and diminished spiritual abilities.

kalpa–sacred law, a period of time, a twelve hour period (a day) of Brahmā said to last one thousand *mahā-yuga* cycles.

karma–derived from the Sanskrit root *kṛ* meaning to do, to make. The work *karma* means action, work, and deed. Only secondarily does *karma* refer to the result of past deeds, which are more properly known as the *phalam* or fruit of action.

karma-yoga–the spiritual path of connecting one's self to God through action or work.

kṣatriya–a member of the traditional military or warrior class. A king, a prince. The *kṣatriya* was the second *varṇa* in the system of *varṇāśrama-dharma.*

kṣara–something that is perishable, the body, the world.

kṣetra–a field, the body, the world.

kṣetra-jña–the knower of the field, the soul, God.

līlā–divine pastime, play of God.

mahā-yuga–a period of time comprised of one cycle of the four *yugas: satya, tretā, dvāpara* and *kali*, a total of 4,320,000 years.

mantra–a Vedic hymn or sacred prayer.

māyā–a trick, illusion.

mokṣa–liberation or freedom of rebirth. *Mokṣa* is one of the four *puruśārthas* or "goals of life," the others being *dharma, artha* and *kāma.*

mukti–see *mokṣa*.

muni–a sage, a silent one.

nirguṇa–without attributes, refers to God conceived to be impersonal.

nirvāṇa–blown out or extinguished as in the case of a lamp. *Nirvāṇa* is generally used to refer to a material life that has been extinguished, one who has achieved freedom from re-birth. The term *nirvāṇa* is commonly used in Buddhism as the final stage a practitioner strives for. The word does not mean heaven.

om–a sacred syllable, the sound of *brahman*, a sound vibrated at the beginning and end of Vedic recitation, the Vedas.

pāpa–literally, *pāpa* is what brings one down. Sometimes translated as sin or evil.

paramātman–the supreme soul, the supersoul, the lord of the heart, an aspect of God that pervades all things.

paramparā–one following the other, the chain of teachers and disciples.

pitṛ–a father, a forefather, an ancestor, a class of celestial beings, the manes.

prakṛti–material nature. In *sāṅkhya* philosophy *prakṛti* is comprised of eight elements: earth, water, fire, air, space, mind, intellect and ego. It is characterized by the three *guṇas*: *sattva*, *rajas* and *tamas*. *Prakṛti* is female. *Puruṣa* is male.

prāṇa–breath, life force, the senses.

prasāda–favor, mercy, blessing, God's blessings, any item that has been offered to God during worship, especially food.

puṇya–the opposite to *pāpa*. *Puṇya* is what elevates; it is virtue or moral merit. *Pāpa* and *puṇya* go together as negative and positive "credits." One reaps the reward of these negative or positive credits in life. The more *puṇya* one cultivates the higher one rises in life, whereas *pāpa* will cause one to find a lower position. *Puṇya* leads to happiness, *pāpa* leads to suffering.

puruṣa–man, male. In *sāṅkhya* philosophy *puruṣa* denotes the Supreme Male Principle in the universe. Its counterpart is *prakṛti*.

puruṣottama–comprised of two words: *puruṣa* + *uttama* literally meaning "highest man." *Puruṣottama* means God.

rajas–the second of the three *guṇas* of matter. Sometimes translated as passion, the phase of *rajas* is characterized by action, passion, creation, etc.

ṛta–what is proper, right, true, divine law.

ṛtu–season, a period of time, menstruation period.

ṛṣi–an inspired poet or sage, a class of beings distinct from men and gods who were the "seers" of the Vedas.

saṅkhya–calculating, enumeration, analysis, categorization. Modern science can be said to be a form of *saṅkhya* because it attempts to analyze and categorize matter into its constituent elements. *Sāṅkhya* (first *a* long) refers to an ancient system of philosophy attributed to the sage Kapila. This philosophy is so called because it enumerates or analyses reality into a set number of basic elements, similar to modern science.

saguṇa–literally, "with attributes," God conceived as possessing humanlike qualities.

śaiva–a follower of Śiva.

śākta–a follower of Durgā (*śakti*).

śakti–power, energy conceived as female in nature.

samādhi–meditative trance, absorption in the divine.

sannyāsī–one situated in the final stage (*āśrama*) of life, a mendicant.

sannyāsa–the fourth or final stage (*āśrama*) of life, characterized by full renunciation.

śāstra–an order, command, rule, scriptural injunction, sacred writings, science, any department of knowledge.

sat–being, good, virtuous, chaste, the third word of the famous three words: *oṃ tat sat,* refers to what is truly real, eternal and permanent, used to mean God or the soul.

sattva–the first of the three *guṇas* of matter. Sometimes translated as goodness, the phase of *sattva* is characterized by lightness, peace, cleanliness, knowledge, etc.

satyam–truth. The word *satyam* is formed from *sat* with the added abstract suffix *ya*. *Sat* refers to what is true and real. The abstract suffix *ya* means "ness." Thus *satyam* literally means trueness or realness.

satya-yuga–the first of the four *yugas*, said to comprise 1,728,000 years, characterized by virtue, wisdom and spirituality.

śloka–a hymn or verse of praise, a stanza or verse in general, a stanza in *anuṣṭubh* metre (the most common metre used in Sanskrit consisting for 4 lines of 8 syllables), fame.

smṛti–literally, "what is heard," the division of the Vedas written by human beings (*pauruṣeya*), comprised of the later tradition that includes the *Mahābhārata*, *Rāmāyana*, *Purāṇas* etc.

śruti–literally, "what is heard," the division of the Vedas not written by human beings (*apauruṣeya*), said to be "heard" by the *ṛṣis*, comprised of the four Vedas including the *Upaniṣads*.

śūdra–a member of the traditional working class. The śūdra was the fourth *varṇa* in the system of *varṇāśrama-dharma*.

sukha–happiness, pleasure.

sura–a godly one, a god, one who follows the path of the Vedas.
svāmī–controller, a *yogī*, one in the renounced stage of life, a *guru*.
tamas–the third of the three *guṇas* of matter. Sometimes translated as darkness, the phase of *tamas* is characterized by darkness, ignorance, slowness, destruction, heaviness, disease, etc.
tapas–heat, voluntary acceptance of trouble for a spiritual goal, austerity, penance.
tapasya–see *tapas*.
tretā-yuga–the second of the four *yugas*, said to last 1,296,000 years.
tyāga–abandonment, renunciation, the performance of actions without attachment to the results of action.
vaikuṇṭha–literally, "without anxiety," the realm or heaven of Viṣṇu.
vairāgya–renounciation, detachment from the world.
vaiṣṇava–a follower of Viṣṇu.
vaiśya–a member of the traditional mercantile or business community. The *vaiśya* was the third *varṇa* in the system of *varṇāśrama-dharma*.
vānaprastha–the third order (*āśrama*) of life, the retired stage. Literally, "one who remains in the forest."
varṇāśrama–the traditional social system of four *varṇas* and four *aśramas*. The word *varṇa* literally means, "color" and it refers to four basic natures of mankind: *brāhmaṇa*, *kṣatriya*, *vaiśya* and *śūdra*. The *āśramas* are the four stages of an individual's life: *brahmacarya* (student), *gṛhastha* (householder), *vanaprastha* (retired) and *sannyāsa* (renounced).
veda(s)–knowledge, the sacred knowledge of the āryans, the Hindu scriptures, the *Ṛg, Yajur, Sāma, Atharva*, the

Mahābhārata, *Rāmāyaṇa*, *Purāṇas*, *Vedānta-sūtra*, etc.
vidyā–knowledge, the goddess Sarasvatī.
vijñāna–derived from the prefix *vi* added to the noun *jñāna*. The prefix *vi* added to a noun tends to diminish or invert the meaning of a word. If *jñāna* is spiritual knowledge, *vijñāna* is practical or profane knowledge. Sometimes *vijñāna* and *jñāna* are used together in the sense of knowledge and wisdom.
viśiṣṭādvaita–often translated as "oneness of the organic unity" or "differentiated monism," the theology taught by the Śrī Vaiṣṇavism associated with Rāmānuja.
viśva-rūpa–God's cosmic form, the universal form, the vision seen by Arjuna in *Bhagavad Gītā* Chapter Eleven.
yajña–sacrifice, the worship of God performed with fire.
yoga–derived from the Sanskrit root *yuj*, to join, to unite, to attach. The English word yoke is cognate with the Sanskrit word *yoga*. We can think of *yoga* as the joining of the *ātman* with the *paramātman*, the soul with God. There are numerous means of joining with God: through action, *karma-yoga*; through knowledge, *jñāna-yoga*; through devotion, *bhakti-yoga*; through meditation, *dhyāna-yoga*, etc. *Yoga* has many other meanings. For example, in astronomy and astrology it refers to a conjunction (union) of planets.
yogī–literally, one possessed of *yoga*. A *yogī* is a practitioner of *yoga*.
yuga–a period of time said to comprise 432,000 years, one of the four ages that rotate like calendar seasons.

Index

A

actions, 139, 144, 149, 154
Advaita Vedanta, 124n
agni-hotra, see fire sacrifice
ancestors (forefathers), 1n, 33, 41, 42, 88n, 99, 103
ancestoral rites, 135-137
asat (unreal), xxxviii-xxxix, 68n, 116n
asuras, see demons
ātmā, (self, soul)
  exists throughout, 157
  essence of being, 124-135
  immortal, 160-165
  knowledge of self, 84n
  mind is, 138
  seen in the eye, 86-87, 168-176
  universal soul, 104-111
  within heart, 61-62
austerity, 43, 67, 102

B

Baka Dalbhya, 7
boon, 9
brahma
  Advaita Vedanta, 124
  all this indeed is, 61-62
  as a bridge, 164-165
  ātmā, 169-176
  city of, 159-163
  four parts, 78-83
  four pillars of, 68-70
  immortality, 44
  infinite, 18n
  om, 50n
  one who understands, 136-150
  path to, 87-88
  seeker of, 24
  space, 59
brahmacārī, 42n
brāhmana, xxxvii , 16, 100
breath,
  composition of the body, 122-125
  consumes al things, 74-75
  foundation of life, 22
  five vital breaths, 110-113
  greater than hope, 150-151
  life-force, 4
  in-breath, 8, 58
  is the concluding chant, 35
  hiṅ, 30
  main, 5-6, 11
  pillar of *brahma*, 68-69, 81-83

C

Campbell, Joseph, xxxvii
charity, 43, 67, 103
compassion, 2, 164-155
consciousness, 138n
creation, 117, 138n

D

Darwin, Charles, xxix
death, 5, 10, 33-34, 43-47, 63-67, 125, 160
demons, (*asuras*) 3-5, 168n,170
desire, 9, 15, 61-62, 67, 160-163, 175
devas, see gods
dharma, 2n, 43-44, 137, 143
directions, 63, 68-69
disease, 65-66, 158
dreams, 70, 97-98, 167, 171-173

E

evil, 3-5, 13, 104, 137, 160, 164, 168, 175
eye, 5, 14-15, 59, 87, 168-169

F

falsehoods, 137, 143
fasting, 66n, 165
father, 82n, 150, 161
fear, 7, 163
fearless, 10-11, 169-173
fire sacrifice (*agni-hotra*), xxxiv-xxxvii, 1n, 12, 164n
forefathers, see ancestors
food, 20-24, 121-125, 145-146
form, 52-58, 116, 118, 176
funerary rites, 62n, 87, 170

G

Gandharva, 41
gāyatrī, 35, 57-59, 64-64, 90n
greatness, 96, 142
gods (*devas*), 1-3, 10-13, 32, 52-56, 88-91, 170-173
gotra (paternal lineage), 76

H

havan, see fire sacrifice
hearing, 68-69, 74, 93-95, 175
heart, 57-62, 158-159, 163,
166-167
High Chant, 1-15, 19-23, 26-42
homa, see fire sacrifice
hope, 42, 70, 149-150, 157
human condition, 88
human beings, 137, 143

I

initiation (*dikṣā*), 67
infallible, 67
ignorance, 3, 131
immortal, 10, 155, 170-173
immortality, 42-44, 167
imperishable, 67
Indra, 42-43, 168-174

J

joy, 70, 83, 101, 157

K

King Soma, 100, 103
knowledge (*vidyā*), 2, 57, 85-87, 114, 165

L

language, xxxvi, 56n, 149
lightning, 27, 85, 100, 103, 120, 147-148, 174
law, 20n, 160

M

man,
  course of, 102
  is a fire, 101
  is a sacrifice, 64, 67
  light within, 61
  power, 144
  sacrifice to create world, 58n
  shackled, 133
  with children, 111-114
  with the cart, 71-73
Manu, 57, 176
māyā, xxxix, 162n
meditation, 110n, 140n, 157
mind, 5, 14, 89, 93-95, 123-125, 138-140, 157
moon, 13, 24, 88, 96, 103, 175
mortal, 155, 164, 174

N

non-existence (*sat*), 116
non-being (*sat*), 68n
non-violence, 67

O

oblations, 42
Om,
  as the High Chant, 1-3
  power of, 9-11
  as the sun and breath, 11
outcastes, 104

P

pāpa, 36
paramātmā, 159n
path to *brahma*, 87-88
path of sacrifice, 88-89, 103
power, 49-51, 95-96, 144-145
Prajapati,
  chant of, 42-44
  Lord of Creatures, 168-176
  offspring, 32
  sound *hiṃ*, 24
  the creator, 89
prāṇa (life force), 4-7, 59, 82n, 94n, 96n, 111
procreate, 66n

R

rasa, 6
real, see *sat*
religion of affirmation, xxxvii-xxxviii
restraint, 187-188
Rudras, 45-46, 53, 65

S

sat (real), xxxviii-xxxix, 68n, 116n, 123-125
semen, 101-103
senses,
  ātmā manifests, 61
  gods disciplined, 2
  prāṇa, 82
  rooted in body, 57
  the best, 93-96
sexual intercourse, 36
sight, 68-69, 74, 93-95, 175
sleep, 74, 123, 162n, 167, 173
Smith, Wilford Cantwell, xxviii
soma, 1n, 26n, 45-47, 64-67, 106
soul, 114-117, 124-133, 175
space, 18-19, 59-60, 82-83, 108, 148-149, 159
speech, 2, 56-59, 89, 93-95, 137
sun, 7-9, 11, 13, 15, 23, 26, 31-34, 37, 49-59, 103, 107, 166-167

T

Theory of evolution, xxix
thought, 94, 115, 140-141, 157
truth, 77, 124n, 137, 143, 152-153, 163

U

universe, 57, 110n, 116n, 159n, 166n
unreal, see *asat*

V

Varuna, 24, 53-54, 62
Vasus, 45, 52, 65
Vedanta, 124n, 162n
Vedas, 2, 10-12, 44, 135-137
Vishvadevas, 45-47

W

wealth, 57-59, 63, 97, 154n
woman, 36, 97-98, 101

Y

Yama, god of death, 62n, 174n

Z

zenith, 34n, 55-56

Twelve Essential Upanishads

Three Volume Series

English translation with annotations

Shukavak N. Dasa

ISBN 978-1-889756-00-4

Volume I

Brihad Aranyaka Upanishad:
The Forest Teachings

Volume II

Chandogya Upanishad:
Teachings from the High Chant

Volume III

Taitiriya, Aitareya, Kaushitaki, Kena, Katha, Isha, Shvetashvatara, Mundaka, Prashna, and Mandukya Upanishads

ISBN 978-1-889756-33-2

ISBN 978-1-889756-04-2

Ganga Flows West
A Hindu Primer

An easy to read and simple explanation of the most important points of Hinduism.

by Shukavak N. Dasa

"I've seen that ritual a hundred times, this however, is the first time I understood its meaning"

Hindu Encounter with Modernity

Kedarnath Datta Bhaktivinoda, Vaiṣṇava Theologian

Nineteen century India was a time of great religious and cultural change as European religions and philosophies spread throughout the Indian subcontinent. Through the eyes of one Hindu religious reformer, Kedarnath Datta Bhaktivinoda, *Hindu Encounter with Modernity* is a study of how Hinduism evolved and adapted to Western culture and ideas.

Bhaktivinoda's life straddled contemporary British society and ancestral Hindu culture. One was a modern, analytical world which demanded rational thought. The other was a traditional world of Hindu faith and piety, which seemingly allowed little room for critical analysis. Could he play a meaningful role in modern society and at the same time maintain integrity as a Hindu? ISBN 978-1-889756-30-1

www.ingramcontent.com/pod-product-compliance
Lightning Source LLC
Chambersburg PA
CBHW041306110526
44590CB00028B/4256
* 9 7 8 1 8 8 9 7 5 6 3 3 2 *